Seasons to Celebrate

January to Summer

Written by Ann Richmond Fisher

Illustrated by Becky J. Radtke

Teaching & Learning Company

1204 Buchanan St., P.O. Box 10
Carthage, IL 62321-0010

This book belongs to

_____

Cover art by Becky J. Radtke

Cover design by Jennifer Morgan

Copyright © 2003, Teaching & Learning Company

ISBN No. 1-57310-408-6

Printing No. 987654321

Teaching & Learning Company
1204 Buchanan St., P.O. Box 10
Carthage, IL 62321-0010

Before offering any food to your students, make sure you are aware of any allergies or dietary restrictions your students may have.

At the time of publication every effort was made to insure the accuracy of the information included in this book. However, we cannot guarantee that agencies and organizations mentioned will continue to operate or to maintain these current locations.

Table of Contents

January

February

March

April

Summer

Dear Teacher or Parent,

Congratulations on choosing part two of the best one-stop seasonal resource ever! Packed inside this volume is a huge assortment of learning activities, bulletin board ideas, recipes and everything you need to celebrate lots of special days from January through summer. This book will supply you with material for many, many special days from New Year's Day to summer vacation. In addition to all the major holidays such as Valentine's Day and St. Patrick's Day, we've also included helps for other special occasions that are just as fun but not as celebrated. For instance, wouldn't your students just love to observe Pancake Day, National Bubble Week and Little League Baseball Week?

While your primary students are enjoying holidays and special observances, they will also be practicing important skills in language, math and other subjects. You'll find many skill-based reproducibles inside that are ready to use. The wide variety of formats used includes puzzles, matching, creative writing, word searches and more. Most require no special supplies or equipment. Additionally, you'll find bulletin board ideas, shape book patterns, party suggestions, parent letters, recipes, songs, poems and much, much more.

An extra-unique feature of this book is the CD-Rom. This helpful aid is packed with lots of whimsical clip art to complement the material inside the book. The clip art is made available in both black-and-white and color and can easily be sized to fit your needs—from name tags, to book covers to special projects. You will also find patterns for bulletin boards, theme-decorated stationery and much, much more! And everything is numbered for easy use and reference.

This large volume is divided into five monthly sections. Most months feature six special occasions. There are language and math pages for each occasion as well as other skill-based materials. Each month includes two or three bulletin board ideas that are complete with patterns and display ideas. Near the end of each monthly section, you'll find award certificates and bookmarks for the units in that month. At the back of the book, you'll also find a handy answer key for the puzzles and activities.

Indeed, there are many seasons to celebrate, and we want to make it easy for you and your students to enjoy them all!

Sincerely,

Ann

Ann Richmond Fisher

January

Get ready for a jolly January! Here is a fresh assortment of bulletin boards, teacher helps and curriculum reproducible pages to see you through many of the special days in January.

We've chosen six special themes: the New Year; Oatmeal Month; Letter-Writing Week; Martin Luther King, Jr. Day; the birthday of Benjamin Franklin and National Puzzle Day. For some of these themes you will find bulletin boards, parent letters and resource lists. For others you might see a song, a student game idea or a poem. For all of the units you will have appealing reproducibles that cover important primary skills. Most skill sheets are for math or language, but we've also included some pages for science, social studies and general thinking skills.

Pick the themes you are most interested in and select activities and worksheets that are on an appropriate level for your students. You will be able to use many ideas in each unit even though some individual pages may be too difficult or too simple for your particular class. You can copy the reproducible pages directly from the book. The bulletin board patterns, stationery and other items are included on the CD and numbered for easy reference.

First, your students will welcome in the New Year by making their own resolutions. They can also solve a maze, work with rhyming words and sharpen their vocabulary.

During Oatmeal Month, your students can learn interesting facts about this nutritious food. These are included on the teacher page and in a reading activity. Of course, you'll want to have your students cooking and eating, so there are recipes and lots of topping ideas, too. Several math activities are also included here.

Letter-writing is strongly encouraged in the third section. On these pages you'll find a bulletin board idea, complete with patterns. There are forms for writing short notes and a practice page for writing a longer letter. Students will also address envelopes and calculate postage costs.

Your students will love learning about Benjamin Franklin as they play a board game, conduct science activities and listen to you read from a list of recommended resource books. They'll also correct math problems, spot differences and identify proper nouns.

National Puzzle Day completes the special themes. Your students can make their own take-home puzzle book, finish a dot-to-dot and solve other fun riddles.

Don't forget all the great clip art on the CD. It promises to make for a truly jolly January in your classroom!

Happy New Year!

Welcome students back to a brand-new year with these fresh-start ideas:

- Sing "Happy New Year to You" to the tune of "Happy Birthday." Let students make up different words for the last line such as "Have a good one, Let's be friends," etc.

- Use the reproducible on page 9 to help students make New Year's resolutions for their conduct or work at school. Explain that a resolution is a decision to improve oneself, and it takes hard work and perseverance to accomplish that goal. Encourage students to write resolutions that are measurable and attainable.

- Calendar-Count: Even if you are already counting up to your 100th day of school, your class can also begin a count of the number of days in the new year. In the bottom corner of each day on a large wall calendar, write a small numeral. Of course, it's easy for January since the numeral written by you (or a student) will match the date already printed there. When February arrives, however, the numbers will be different. Lead students to see throughout the year that the numeral written in each day is the sum of the total number of days in the preceding months, plus the number of days that have passed so far in the current month. For example, they should understand that March 10th is the 69th day of the year, since January has 31 days, February has 28 and 10 days have passed in the current month. (31 + 28 + 10 = 69). Leap year, naturally, adds one more day.

- Talk about *old* and *new.* Use the reproducible on page 11 to aid your discussion. Look around the classroom for things that are old and new. Ask each student to bring in one thing from home that is new and one thing that is old. (Be sure each child has his family's permission.)

- Challenge students to find other opposites in the classroom as well. Possibilities include: light/dark, noisy/quiet, hard/soft, left/right, up/down, over/under, open/closed and many more.

- Use page 12 to talk about rhyming words. Before giving the students the assignment on the page, work together to list words that rhyme with *old,* such as *cold, fold* and *sold.* (See if anyone lists *rolled*!) Point out that while rhyming words often share the same last letters, that is not always the case. Then start listing words that rhyme with *new.* Here there are many more words with different spellings, such as *moo, do* and *blue.* Some of these are included in the story on page 12.

- Use some *new* things of your own to spark the children's interest: new reward stickers, new bulletin boards, new snack foods and perhaps a new classroom routine or two!

Resolution Form

Use with suggestions found on page 8.

I hereby resolve to

_____

beginning today!

I understand that I will have to work hard every day to meet this goal.
I am counting on my teacher and family members to help me.

_____
Signed

_____
Signed

_____
Family member

_____
Date

Name _____

Happy New Year!

Help Jena get to her New Year's party. She needs to pick up 6 party hats along the way for herself and her friends. Draw a path through the maze so that Jena can find 6 hats on her way to the party.

Name _____

Old and new
What's New?

In each row of pictures, find the objects that are new and color them.
Put an X on the things that are old.

Name _____

A New Rhyme

Listen to this story while your teacher reads it, or you may read it for yourself.
Find the words that rhyme with *new* in this story. Underline all the words you find,
even if you find the same word more than once.

Remember, words that rhyme are not always spelled with the same letters. For
example, *new* and *too* have the same ending sound, although they are spelled
with different letters.

"Hi, Sue!" said Lou. "What's new with you?"

The children were back to school after their winter holiday.

"Lou," said Sue, "I received the nicest gifts. Mom and Dad gave me a

blue sweater. Gram gave me two free tickets to the zoo. Uncle Drew gave me the

game, Clue™.   Do you want to tell me what your family gave to you?

Before Sue could answer, their teacher asked them to line up to go to the library.

Mrs. Woo said, "It's time to return our books today. Be sure to bring all of your library

books with you. Some of you have some that are overdue. Before we leave, Kate,

please glue the torn cover on your book. And, Alex, be sure to tie your left shoe."

Later that day Sue and Lou finished their chat about their holidays. Both agreed

the New Year was off to a very good start.

Did you find 35 words? If not, look again and underline more words that rhyme with
new.

Name _____

New News!

How quickly can you fill in the blanks on this page?
You will need to finish spelling an answer for each clue. Use the word box for help.

1. Something that is printed new every day for you and your family to read

   n e w s ___ ___ ___ ___ ___

2. a baby that's just been born   n e w ___ ___ ___ ___

3. someone who's just been married   n e w ___ ___ ___ ___ ___

4. the first holiday of the year   N e w ___ ___ ___ ___ ' ___   ___ ___ ___

5. a small printed leaflet with important information

   n e w ___ ___ ___ ___ ___ ___ ___

6. someone who has just arrived   n e w ___ ___ ___ ___ ___

7. one of our 50 states   N e w ___ ___ ___ ___ ___ ___

8. paper made from ground wood pulp and used mostly for newspaper

   n e w ___ ___ ___ ___ ___ ___

9. the night before January 1   N e w ___ ___ ___ ___ ' ___   ___ ___ ___

10. a television or radio broadcast of news   n e w ___ ___ ___ ___ ___

New Year's Day   newspaper   newcomer
New Year's Eve   New Jersey   newsletter
newsprint   newborn
newlywed   newscast

Oatmeal Month

Did you know that more oatmeal is sold during January than during any other month? Or did you know that 80% of U.S. households stock oatmeal in their cupboards? Learn more about this nutritious cereal *and* give your students practice in important language and math skills, too, by using the pages in this section.

Begin by looking through the recipes on pages 15, 16 and 25. After reading through these recipes (as well as the basic recipe on this page), choose the ones you want to make with your students during the month of January. You may decide to cook together more than once this month! Also look at the lists of oatmeal toppings on pages 21 and 22. Choose some of these to eat on plain hot oatmeal. After you've made your selections, note the ingredients you'll need and the dates on which you'll need them. Insert this information into the family letter shown on page 17. Then get ready to collect the donated foods and stir up some tasty, nutritious fun!

Here are instructions for basic oatmeal:

Microwave: For 1 serving, combine $1/3$ cup quick-cooking oats with $2/3$ cup water in a 2-cup microwave-safe bowl. Microwave on *HIGH* for about 1-2 minutes. Stir. Then let stand for 1-2 minutes or until it reaches desired consistency.

Stovetop: (Use the same ratio of oats to water as in microwave recipe, about $1/3$ cup oats to $2/3$ cup water for each serving.) First bring water to a full rolling boil. Then add oats. Reduce heat to a medium setting and cook for 1 minute, stirring frequently. Cover and remove from heat. Let stand 2-3 minutes before serving.

Note: Because you can use a large saucepan and cook many servings at once, the stovetop method is preferable if cooking for a large group of students.

Sometime during the month, be sure to visit the web site of the Quaker Oats company at www.quakeroatmeal.com. Here you will find fun facts, nutritional news and lots more recipes.

Oatmeal Recipes

There's something here for every taste—and classroom.
Recipes are prepared in different ways with different ingredients.
Look them over carefully, then decide which one you'll be tasting first!

Easy Oat Treats
Makes about 4 dozen.

1 cup peanut butter
1 cup powdered sugar
1/2 cup milk
1 teaspoon vanilla
2 cups oats (quick or old-fashioned, uncooked)
2 cups in all of raisins, chocolate or butter-scotch baking chips, and chopped peanuts*

Combine peanut butter, sugar, milk and vanilla. Mix well. Add oats and other ingredients. Drop by rounded teaspoonfuls onto trays lined with waxed paper. Let stand until firm. Store in tightly covered containers.

*Coconut, dried fruit, m&m's® or Reese's® Pieces may also be used.

Peanut Butter Oatmeal Clusters
Makes about 3 dozen.

2 cups sugar
1/2 cup milk
8 tablespoons (1 stick) margarine
1 teaspoon vanilla
3 cups oats

Combine sugar, margarine and milk in large saucepan. Bring to a full boil, and continue boiling for 1 minute. Remove from heat. Add vanilla and peanut butter. Stir until smooth. Add oats and mix well. Drop by rounded teaspoonfuls onto trays lined with waxed paper. Chill until firm. Store tightly covered.

Oatmeal Molasses Oven Cookies

Divide students into four groups. Instruct each group to complete one part of these directions. Makes about 3 dozen.

1. Sift or mix together gently:
   3/4 cup flour
   1/2 cup sugar
   2 teaspoons baking powder
   1/2 teaspoon salt
   2 teaspoons baking soda
   1 teaspoon cinnamon
   1/2 teaspoon cloves

2. Combine:
   2 1/2 cups quick-cooking oats
   1 cup raisins
   Add these to the flour mixture.

3. Combine in a separate bowl:
   2/3 cup melted shortening
   1 egg, beaten
   3/4 cup molasses
   1 tablespoon milk

4. Pour the egg mixture over the dry mixture. Mix well. Drop by teaspoonfuls on greased baking sheet. Bake at 350°F for 15 minutes.

More Oatmeal Recipes

Oats aren't just for cookies. Take a look at these tasty treats!

Microwave Peach Crisp

Makes about 6 servings.

3 cups sliced fresh peaches (about 4 medium peaches)

Or

2 cans, 16 oz. each, of sliced peaches, drained
1/2 cup quick-cooking oats
1/2 cup baking mix (such as Bisquick®)
1/2 cup packed brown sugar
3 tablespoons softened margarine
1/2 teaspoon ground cinnamon
1/2 teaspoon ground nutmeg

Arrange the peaches in an 8" x 8" microwavable dish. Mix together remaining ingredients until crumbly. Sprinkle over peaches. Microwave on high uncovered for 6 minutes. Rotate dish. Microwave until peaches are tender, about 4-6 minutes longer. Serve with ice cream or whipped cream if desired.

Make-Your-Own Granola

Makes about 5 1/2 cups.

3 1/2 cups oats (quick or old fashioned, uncooked)
1/3 cup chopped nuts, optional
1/2 cup honey
4 tablespoons (1/2 stick) melted margarine
1 teaspoon vanilla
1/2 teaspoon ground cinnamon
1 cup raisins or other dried fruit

Preheat oven to 350°F. Mix oats and nuts. Spread evenly in large, rimmed baking sheet. In small bowl, combine honey, margarine, vanilla and cinnamon. Mix well. Pour over oats, and mix again. Bake for 30 minutes or until golden brown, stirring every 10 minutes. Stir in raisins. Cool completely. Store tightly covered for up to 1 week.

Oatmeal Banana Pancakes

Makes about 3 dozen.

2 large bananas, peeled and sliced
1 tablespoon granulated sugar
1 cup flour
1/2 cup oats, quick or old-fashioned, uncooked
1/4 teaspoon ground cinnamon
1 cup milk
1 egg, slightly beaten
2 tablespoons vegetable oil
pancake syrup, warmed

Combine banana slices and sugar. Stir to coat slices, then set aside. In large mixing bowl, combine flour, oats, baking powder, cinnamon and salt. In a separate smaller bowl, mix together milk, egg and oil. Blend well. Add the milk mixture to the dry ingredients. Stir just until all ingredients are moistened. Do not overmix. Preheat griddle or electric skillet to 350°F. Lightly grease skillet. For each pancake, pour about 1/4 cup batter onto hot surface. Place 4-5 banana slices for each pancake on top of the batter. When the slices are covered, and when the edges of the batter look cooked, carefully turn the pancakes. Serve with warm syrup.

TLC10408 Copyright © Teaching & Learning Company, Carthage, IL 62321-0010

Date: _____

Dear Parents/Caregivers,

January is Oatmeal Month, and we plan to celebrate! Our class will be learning about this nutritious food, and we will also be cooking together.

Could you help us? We will be needing some special ingredients, cooking utensils and volunteers. Here is the ingredient I would like you to furnish:

_____

We will need to have this at school on or before _____ .

Also, if you can spare any of these utensils for a few days, we'd be most grateful:

_____

_____

Finally, if you can help us cook, we'll let you sample our treats. The days when we will most need help are

_____ .

Please let me know if you are available.

Please phone or write if you have any questions. As always, thank you very much for your help and cooperation.

Here's to a healthy New Year,

_____
Signed

P.S. If you have not already done so, please make me aware of any food allergies or dietary restrictions your child may have. I will be glad to share the recipes or discuss this further if you wish. Please let me know.

Visual discrimination

Oatmeal Energy!

These five kids have just enjoyed a hot, tasty bowl of oatmeal for breakfast. They feel so good now that they are turning somersaults! Trace the action line from each bowl of cereal to the child who ate from it. Write the correct child's name on each bowl.

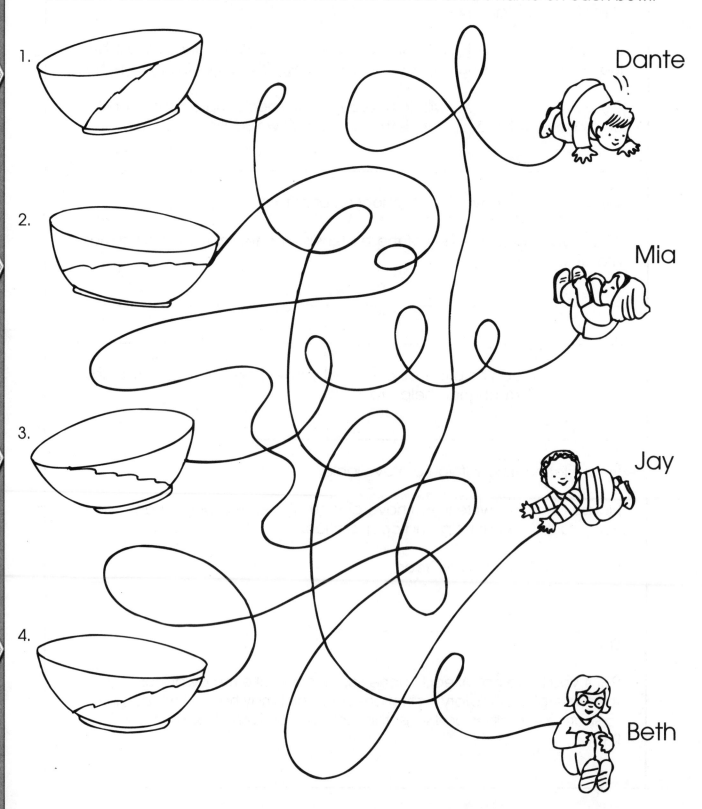

1.

2.

3.

4.

Dante

Mia

Jay

Beth

Name _____

Teacher: For younger students, do this lesson orally. After reading the chart to them two to three times, they should remember the information well enough to answer most of the questions.

Reading comprehension

How Oatmeal Is Made

Read this chart about oatmeal. Then answer the questions below.

1. Oats are grown on a farm.
2. When they are ripe, the oats are picked, usually by a machine.
3. The oats are cleaned to remove the sticks, dust and seeds.
4. The oat grains are dried, or toasted.
5. When the grains of oats are cooled, the *hulls* are removed by a machine, leaving the *groats*.
6. The groats are polished to make them smooth.
7. Next they are softened by steam.
8. The groats are flattened or "rolled" by huge rollers.
9. Finally the rolled oats are packed in containers and sent to food stores.

Write *True* by the true statements and *False* by the untrue statements.

_____ A. Oats are picked from the field and then sent straight to the stores.

_____ B. Hulls are the part of the oat grain that is taken off.

_____ C. The part of the oat grain that we eat in oatmeal is called *groats*.

_____ D. Groats are rolled before they are dried.

_____ E. Groats are softened with steam.

_____ F. Oats are grown in restaurants.

_____ G. Oats are cleaned to remove sticks and dust.

_____ H. Oats are covered with water before the hulls are removed.

_____ I. Flattened oats are also called rolled oats.

Name _____

Long e and long o vowel sounds

Oatmeal Sounds

Can you hear the long o sound in the first part of *oatmeal*? Can you also hear the long e sound in the second part of *oatmeal*? Say the word for each picture below. Each word contains either the long o sound or the long e sound. If you hear the long o sound, circle the word *oat*. If you hear the long e sound, circle the word *meal*.

oat meal	oat meal	oat meal
oat meal	oat meal	oat meal
oat meal	oat meal	oat meal
oat meal	oat meal	oat meal

TLC10408 Copyright © Teaching & Learning Company, Carthage, IL 62321-0010

Name _____

Tasty Toppings

Hot oatmeal can be enjoyed with lots of different toppings.
Here are just 20 popular ideas. Number them from 1 to 20 to show
what comes first, second, third and so on in ABC order.

_____ walnuts

_____ figs

_____ strawberries

_____ raisins

_____ granola

_____ nectarines

_____ jam

_____ pineapple

_____ caramel

_____ almonds

_____ pears

_____ bananas

_____ cranberries

_____ wheat germ

_____ yogurt

_____ dates

_____ pancake syrup

_____ apples

_____ honey

_____ oranges

A. What topping is *your* favorite? _____

B. What topping from the list above would you like to try? _____

C. What other toppings can you name? _____

Solving a word search
More Tasty Toppings

This page contains the names of even more tasty foods you may want to put on top of your hot bowl of oatmeal. Try to find every word on the list. Words may appear up and down, across or diagonally, both backwards and forwards.

almonds
apple
applesauce
apricots
brown sugar
chocolate chips
chopped pecans
cinnamon
dates
figs
granola
honey
kiwi
mashed banana
orange marmalade
peach
peanut butter
pineapple
raisins
raspberries
sliced pears
strawberries
syrup
wheat germ
yogurt

```
O B S N A C E P D E P P O H C
M R R X P U R Y S M I L K S M
A O A S T O C I R P A R I E I
S W E N M R E G T A E H W I L
H N P H G X X R A T X P I R K
E S D O X E U L T S G I F R A
D U E N X G M U X K X N X E P
B G C E O O B A H L S E S B P
A A I Y N T L C R I E A N W L
N R L D U O A X K M T P I A E
A X S N N E M I L K A P S R S
N X A A P P L E I X D L I T A
A E R C I N N A M O N E A S U
P G S E I R R E B P S A R D C
S P I H C E T A L O C O H C E
```

Bonus Challenge: How many times can you find the word *MILK*? _____
Milk is the most popular oatmeal topping of all!

Name _____

Raisin Count

Chef Groats is cooking up a lot of oatmeal for the customers in his restaurant. He wants to be sure that each bowl he serves has exactly 10 raisins on top. He's in a hurry, and you can see that these bowls aren't right. Some have more than 10 raisins and some have less. Can you help? Cross out the extra raisins on the bowls that have too many. Draw more raisins on the bowls than have too few.

Name _____

Telling time to half-hour
Wake Up?

Nine kids all eat their Saturday morning oatmeal at different times. Some get up very early, and some sleep in very late. Look at the names and times below. Draw hands on each clock to match the time each child eats breakfast.

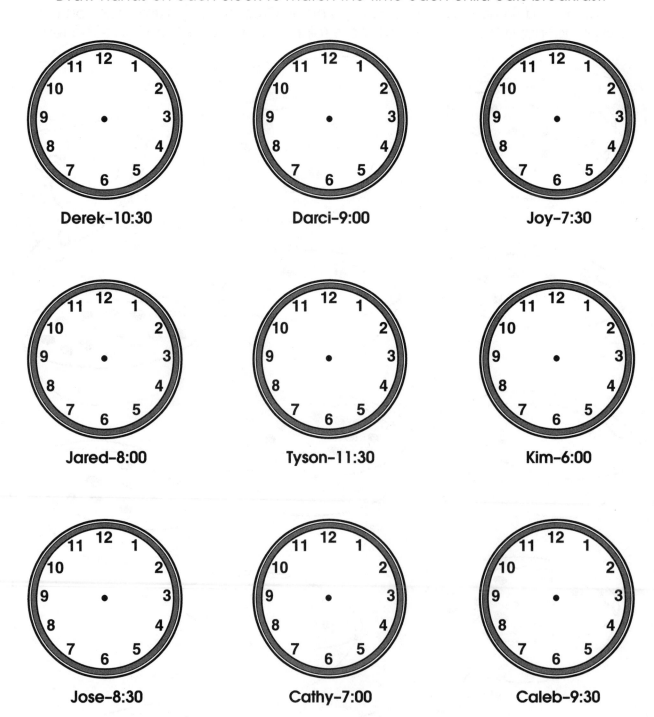

Derek-10:30   **Darci-9:00**   **Joy-7:30**

Jared-8:00   **Tyson-11:30**   **Kim-6:00**

Jose-8:30   **Cathy-7:00**   **Caleb-9:30**

What time do you eat your Saturday morning breakfast?
Draw a clock on the back of this page showing the time.

TLC10408 Copyright © Teaching & Learning Company, Carthage, IL 62321-0010

Name _____

Kitchen Math
Read this recipe carefully. Then answer the questions below.

Chocolate Clusters

2 cups granulated sugar
8 tablespoons (1 stick) margarine
$1/3$ cup milk

$1/3$ cup unsweetened baking cocoa
$3 1/2$ cups oats (quick, uncooked)
1 teaspoon vanilla

Combine sugar, milk, margarine and cocoa in large saucepan. Bring to a boil over medium heat, stirring often. Continue boiling the mixture for about 2 minutes. Remove pan from heat. Stir in oats and vanilla. Drop by tablespoonfuls onto pans that have been lined with waxed paper. Let stand (or chill) until firm. Store in a tightly covered container. Makes about 3 dozen. Note: When adding the oats, 1 cup coconut, raisins or chopped nuts may also be added.

1. How much milk do you need if you want to make:

   a. two batches of Chocolate Clusters? _____

   b. three batches? _____

   c. four batches? _____

   d. six batches? _____

2. How much cocoa is needed for:

   a. two batches? _____

   b. three batches? _____

   c. five batches? _____

3. How many cups of oats are needed for:

   a. two batches? _____

   b. three batches? _____

Letter-Writing Week

Get your students' New Year off to good start by encouraging them to send letters and cards to their friends and relatives. Letter-Writing Week is the second week in January. The bulletin board shown here and the reproducibles on the pages that follow should help you do just that.

Begin Letter-Writing Week with this appealing bulletin board. At the beginning of the week, staple envelopes to the bulletin board which have been addressed to each of your students. Tuck a short letter inside that you have written. (See page 29 for sample stationery.) If you like, allow students to write letters to each other during the week and "deliver" them by posting them on the bulletin board. Again you may use page 29 for letter-writing forms.

Date _____

Dear _____,

_____

_____

_____

_____

_____

_____

_____

Your friend,

_____

Date _____

Dear _____,

_____

_____

_____

_____

_____

Your friend,

_____

Date _____

Dear _____,

I am writing to you because _____

_____

_____

_____

_____

_____

Your friend,

_____

Date _____

Dear _____,

_____

_____

_____

_____

_____

_____

_____

Your friend,

_____

Name _____

Mail Time

Josh is getting ready to send a letter to his cousin. In each row, number
the pictures in order from 1 to 3 to show what comes first, second and third.

30   TLC10408 Copyright © Teaching & Learning Company, Carthage, IL 62321-0010

Name _____

Pen Pal

Pretend you are writing a letter to someone you've never met before. Pretend that this "pen pal" lives in another country and has never visited our country. Think about the most important things you would like to say. Then complete this letter form.

Date

_____
- -
_____
Month   Day   Year

Greeting

Dear Pen Pal,

Body

_____
- -
_____
- -
_____
- -
_____
- -
_____
- -
_____
- -
_____
- -
_____

Signature closing

Your friend,

_____
- -
_____

Writing letters
Funny Lines

Can you write a silly letter? Here are 10 ideas for you. Choose one idea and think of how you could write a letter for it. Then write your letter on another piece of paper, using the correct form as shown on page 31. If you have time, choose a second idea to write about. Be ready to share your letters with your classmates.

Ideas

1. Pretend you are a clown who is writing a letter to a kid who wants to become a clown.

2. Pretend you are a skunk writing a letter to apologize for making someone's home smell badly.

3. Pretend you are a fish writing a letter to a fisherman asking him not to fish in your lake.

4. Pretend you are weather forecaster. You are writing a letter to your boss, telling him you want to quit your job because your forecast is never right.

5. Pretend you are a pair of scissors writing to the hairdresser who has used you to cut hair for the last 20 years. Tell her you are ready to retire.

6. Pretend you are a sidewalk. You want to write a letter to all the kids in the neighborhood asking them to spend more time on your side of the street.

7. Pretend you are a chocolate chip cookie. You need to write a letter to the Smith family giving them at least three good reasons why they should not eat you.

8. Pretend you are a computer keyboard. Write a letter to a 10-year-old asking him not to pound your keys so hard.

9. Pretend you are a snowman. Write a letter to the kids who made you, thanking them for doing such a nice job.

10. Pretend you are a popular singer. Write a letter to a radio station, asking them to play your songs more often.

Addressing envelopes

The Envelope, Please

The envelope is a very important part of letter-writing. The envelope tells where the letter is to be sent. The envelope must be addressed correctly if you want the letter to go to the right place. Follow these directions:

1. Write your name and address in the upper-left corner. This is called the return address. It tells the post office where the letter can be returned if it cannot be delivered to the address given.

2. Put the stamp in the upper-right corner. Make sure you include the right amount of postage.

3. Put the name and address of the person you want to receive the letter in the middle of the envelope. Use your neatest handwriting. Write large enough so that it can be easily read, but small enough so that you can fit all the information in.

4. Be sure to include the street address, city, state and ZIP code.

This is an example of how an envelope should be written. It is being sent from Betsy Fisher, to her grandparents, Mr. and Mrs. Russell Richmond.

Betsy Fisher
1234 My Street
My Town, PA 10000

Mr. and Mrs. Russell Richmond
6789 Their Street
Their Town, MI 00001

Addressing envelopes

The Envelope, Please

Look at this envelope. You can see that it contains several mistakes.
Circle the mistakes that you see. Write the envelope correctly in the bottom box.

IIIII Mill Hall, PA
613 Ohboy St.
Bryce Fisher

Caleb Miller
897 Lee avenue
goshen, in 40000

Finding sums

Stampwork

Did you know that it costs more to send a letter than it does to send a postcard? Also, heavier letters, envelopes that are large and most packages require more postage than regular letters. Pretend that each piece of mail needs to have the amount of postage that's written on it. Circle the correct stamps that will add up to that amount.

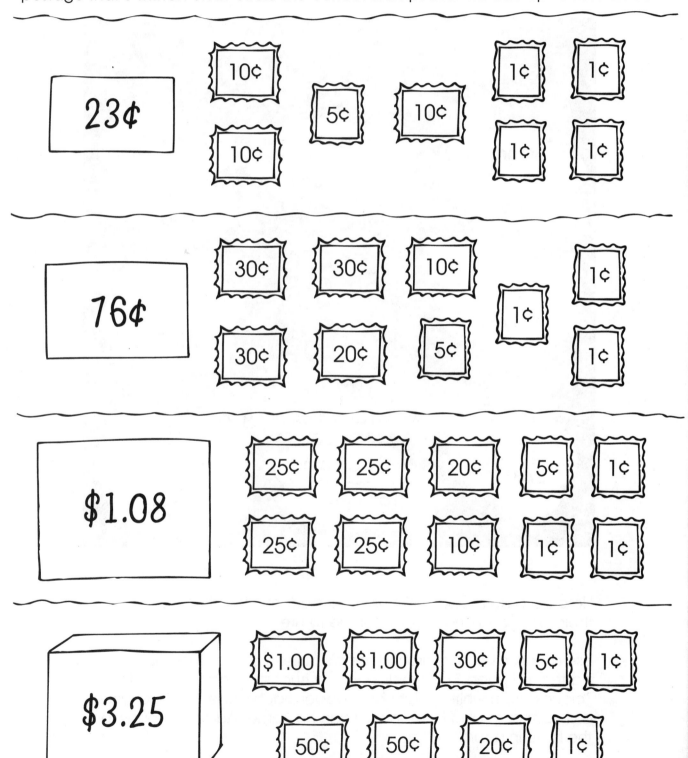

Bulletin board
Martin Luther King, Jr. Day

Here's a bulletin board to help your students start thinking about their own goals and dreams for the future.

Use a dark blue background for this bulletin board. Then use the pattern on page 37 for the center. Instruct students to cut out "clouds" from white or light blue paper. Each student should write a dream or goal of his own and sign his name. Add the clouds to the bulletin board.

36

TLC10408 Copyright © Teaching & Learning Company, Carthage, IL 62321-0010

Martin Luther King, Jr.

Letter recognition

Peace

Martin Luther King, Jr. talked a lot about peace. He believed that people of all colors could live together in peace. Cut out the letter squares on this page. Find the letters that spell *peace* in small letters and glue them together on the top portion of a piece of construction paper. Find all the letters that spell *PEACE* in capital letters. Glue them together on the bottom of the same piece of construction paper. Watch out! There are extra letters that you will not need.

A	F	c	E
V	a	E	p
P	G	e	o
e	C	a	g

Name _____

Sounds Right

Martin Luther King, Jr.'s three initials were M, L and K. Can you hear the sound of each of these letters in the three parts of his name? Look at the picture in each box below. Decide which of the letters, M, L or K, come at the beginning of the word that names the picture. Circle that letter.

m l k	m l k	m l k
m l k	m l k	m l k
m l k	m l k	m l k
m l k	m l k	m l k

Name _____

Just Because

Everything has a cause and an effect. For example, if someone leaves a banana peel
on the floor, you might fall down. The banana peel on the floor is the cause.
Your fall is the effect. Read each problem. Make an X in front of any likely cause.

1. Martin Luther King, Jr. had a dream for a better future because

    a. _____ he wanted to watch more TV.

    b. _____ he had children.

    c. _____ he thought people could get along together better.

2. Martin Luther King planned a march in Washington, D.C., because

    a. _____ a lot of important things happen in Washington, D.C.

    b. _____ he wanted our leaders to see the march.

    c. _____ it was cold.

3. Mrs. King traveled with her husband sometimes because

    a. _____ she agreed with his ideas.

    b. _____ she wanted to go to a restaurant.

    c. _____ she enjoyed spending time with her husband.

Now read each problem, and make an X in front of any likely effect.

4. We had the day off school on Martin Luther King, Jr. Day, so we

    a. _____ slept in.

    b. _____ watched a TV program about MLK.

    c. _____ wore sweaters.

5. Sue was asked to give a speech at school about Martin Luther King, Jr., so she

    a. _____ went to the library to find books about him.

    b. _____ took a shower.

    c. _____ helped cook supper.

6. Mark wanted to learn more about Martin Luther King, Jr., so he

    a. _____ phoned his two-year-old cousin.

    b. _____ read about King on the internet.

    c. _____ rented a video about King's life.

TLC10408 Copyright © Teaching & Learning Company, Carthage, IL 62321-0010

Name _____

What's Next?

Read each story. Think about what will happen next.
Write two sentences to tell what happens next.

A. Joe and Jenny were planning a special program for Martin Luther King, Jr.
Day for their class at school.
"I would like to read a story I wrote about his life," said Joe.
"That sounds great!" said Jenny.
"I think someone should read King's speech called "I Have a Dream," said
Joe.

_____

_____

_____

_____

_____

_____

B. Mom and Dad wanted to plan a special surprise for Martin Luther King, Jr.
Day. They thought about renting a video about King's life. They thought
about getting some books from the library.
"I think we saw a video last year," said Mom.
"I think we read a lot of books about King last year, too," said Dad.
Then Mom remembered that there was a new museum in town. The museum
had a display about Dr. King.

_____

_____

_____

_____

_____

_____

On the back of this page, draw a picture to show one of your predictions.

Sequencing timed events
A Busy Life

What a busy life Dr. Martin Luther King, Jr. must have led! He was a husband, father, pastor and public leader. He probably spent time with his wife, children, church congregation and other African American leaders–maybe all in one day! Suppose that Dr. King did all the things listed below in one day. Look at the time in which he did each one. Number the events from 1 to 14 to show what he did first, second, third and so on.

_____ Martin and his family ate supper together at 5:30 p.m.

_____ He ate breakfast with his wife and children at 7:30 a.m.

_____ At 1:00 p.m., Martin met with other pastors in the community to plan a peaceful march.

_____ Martin visited sick people in the hospital at 9 a.m.

_____ Martin woke up at 6 a.m. and read his Bible, showered and dressed.

_____ Martin picked up his children from school at 3:00 p.m.

_____ Martin went to bed at 11:00 p.m.

_____ Dr. King met with the mayor at 4:00 p.m.

_____ At 10:00 p.m. Martin worked on his sermon and read his Bible again.

_____ He worked on his sermon at 11:30 a.m.

_____ At 8:00 p.m. Martin wrote letters to thank people for helping him with past events.

_____ Martin read his mail and returned phone calls at 9:00 p.m.

_____ At 3:30 p.m., he made phone calls to help plan his next march.

_____ Martin led a prayer service in his church at 6:30 p.m.

Name _____

Martin's March

Here is the map of one city that is planning a special parade for Martin Luther King, Jr. Day. Follow all the directions on the next page to learn what buildings are in this town, and where the parade will be.

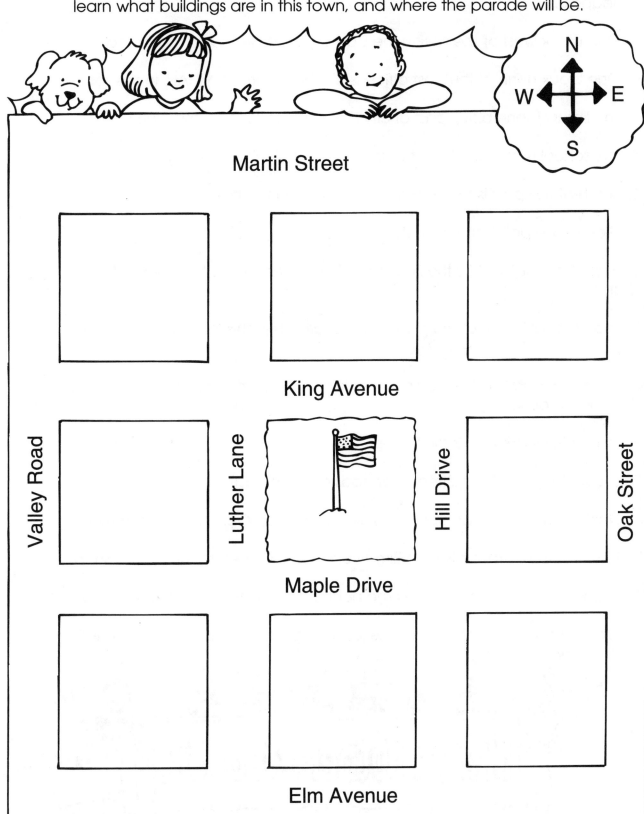

Martin's March

1. The park is the area that includes the flag. Write PARK in the area around the flagpole.

2. One block west of the park is the post office. Write P.O. in this space.

3. One block north of the post office is city hall. Write CITY HALL in this spot.

4. The library is one block east of city hall. Write LIBRARY in this block.

5. The school is one block east of the library. Write SCHOOL in this space.

6. South of the park is the pet shop. Write PETS in the block south of the park.

7. West of the pet shop is a coffee shop. Write COFFEE in this place.

8. East of the pet shop is the zoo. Write ZOO in the block that's east of the pet store.

9. The hospital is east of the park. Write a large H in this last space on your map.

Now find the route for the Martin Luther King, Jr. Day march. Draw in the path that follows these directions:

A. Start at City Hall on Martin Street.

B. Draw a line on Martin Street that goes east, from City Hall to the school.

C. Next the march will go from the school, south on Oak Street to the zoo.

D. From the zoo, draw a line on Elm Avenue going west to the coffee shop.

E. From the coffee shop, draw a line north on Valley Road to King Avenue.

F. Go east on King Avenue from the post office to the park. The march will end at the park.

TLC10408 Copyright © Teaching & Learning Company, Carthage, IL 62321-0010

Resources

Happy Birthday Martin Luther King, Jr. by Jean Marzollo. Scholatstic, 1992.

I Have a Dream by Martin Luther King, Jr. Foreword by Corretta Scott King. Scholastic, 1997.

Martin Luther King, Jr. and the March on Washington by Frances E. Ruffin. Penguin Putnam Books for Young Readers, 2000.

Martin Luther King, Jr. Day by Mir Tamim Ansary. Heinemann Library, 2002.

Martin Luther King, Jr. (Lives and Times) by Peter and Connie Roop. Heinemann Library, 2001.

Martin's Big Words: The Life of Dr. Martin Luther King, Jr. by Doreen Rappaport, et al. Jump at the Sun, 2001.

Meet Martin Luther King, Jr. (Landmark Books) by James Tertius de Kay. Random House, 2001.

My Dream of Martin Luther King by Faith Ringgold. Crown Publishing Group, 1998.

A Picture Book of Martin Luther King, Jr. by David Adler. Holiday House, Inc., 1991.

What Is Martin Luther King, Jr. Day? by Margaret Friskey, et al. Children's Press, 1990.

Young Martin Luther King, Jr: "I Have a Dream" by Joanne Mattern. Troll Communications, 1992.

Dr. Martin Luther King, Jr. Poster Paper by Robynne Eagan. Teaching & Learning Company, 1996.

Birthday of Benjamin Franklin

Benjamin Franklin was born on January 17, 1706. Commemorate this special day in your classroom. Franklin was a great inventor, scientist and statesman, and there is much to be learned from his life. Be sure to read some of the books listed on page 55 to your students.

Here are some highlights from Franklin's life:

1706—Born in Boston, Massachusetts

1718—Apprenticed to his brother, James, a printer

1723—Ran away to Philadelphia to start his own printing press

1732—Published the first edition of his *Poor Richard's Almanac*

1752—Published reports of his experiments with electricity

1776—Helped draft the Declaration of Independence

1776—Traveled to France as a special envoy of the U.S.

1787—Helped write the U.S. Constitution

1790—Died in Philadelphia

Franklin invented bifocals, the Franklin stove, an odometer, the lightning rod and more.

During his lifetime, Franklin was recognized as one of the greatest scientific thinkers in the world. He studied heat conduction and the origin of storms. His most notable work, however, was done with electricity.

His most famous experiment, of course, was the one in which he proved that lightning is electricity. In 1752 he worked on an experiment with the help of his son, William. During a thunderstorm, the two went to a shed in an open meadow. They flew a kite high in the air, and brought a charge of electricity down the kite's wet string. Franklin noticed the loose threads of the kite string standing up. As final proof, Franklin put his knuckle on a key at his end of the string and saw an electric spark. Franklin's book covering his studies on electricity was one of the most widely reprinted scientific books of his time. See pages 53-54 for more information and activities about lightning and electricity.

Encourage your students to learn about Franklin's other writings, experiments, inventions. Use the shape book pattern from page 47 for students to record their new knowledge. Use the skill pages in this section to provide practice with counting, nouns, addition and spotting differences.

Shape Book Pattern

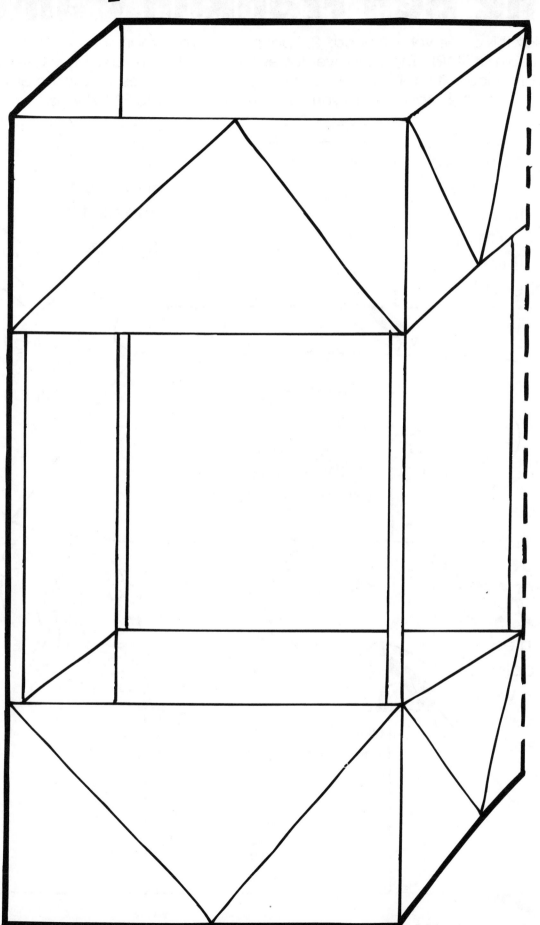

The Ben Franklin Game

To play this game you will need: 2-4 people, a coin, a marker for each person.
Rules: Begin at START. The first player tosses the coin. If it is heads, the player moves ahead 1 space. If it is tails, the player moves ahead 2 spaces. Follow the directions on the space where you land. The first player to FINISH wins.

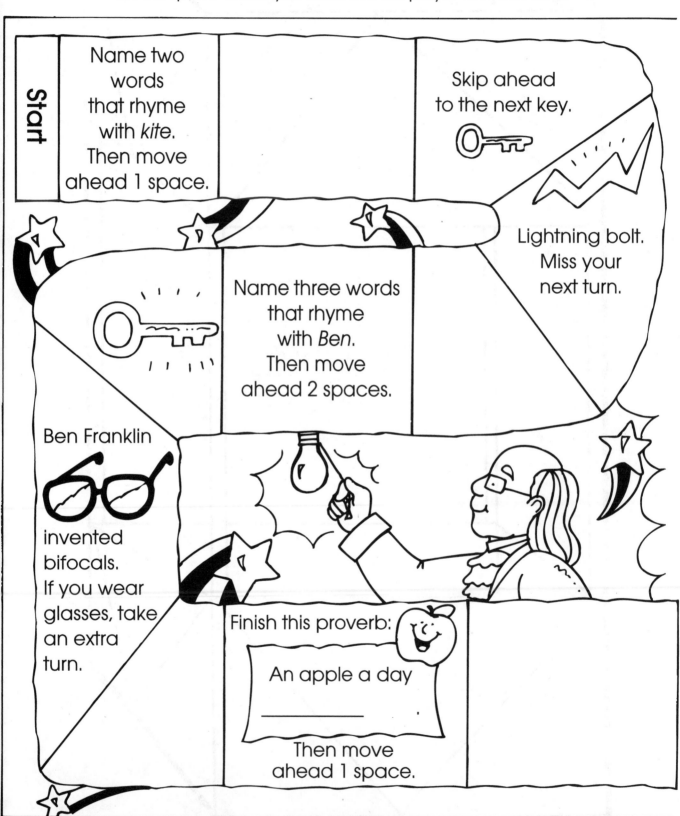

Start

Name two words that rhyme with *kite*. Then move ahead 1 space.

Skip ahead to the next key.

Lightning bolt. Miss your next turn.

Name three words that rhyme with *Ben*. Then move ahead 2 spaces.

Ben Franklin invented bifocals. If you wear glasses, take an extra turn.

Finish this proverb:

An apple a day

_____ .

Then move ahead 1 space.

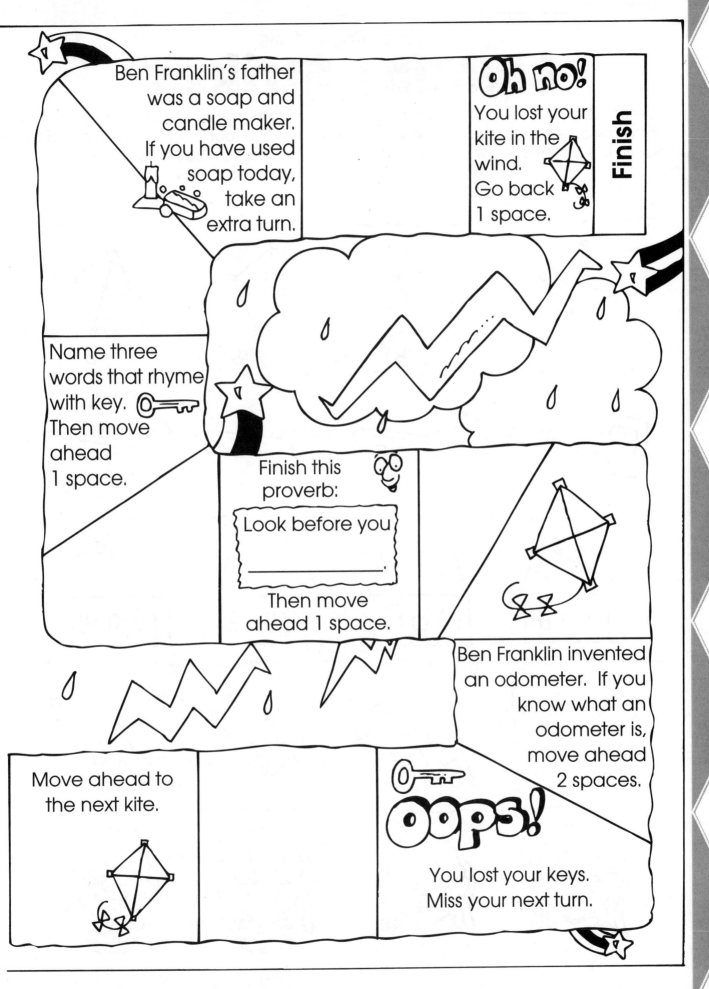

Ben Franklin's father was a soap and candle maker. If you have used soap today, take an extra turn.

Oh no! You lost your kite in the wind. Go back 1 space.

Finish

Name three words that rhyme with key. Then move ahead 1 space.

Finish this proverb:

Look before you _____.

Then move ahead 1 space.

Ben Franklin invented an odometer. If you know what an odometer is, move ahead 2 spaces.

Move ahead to the next kite.

Oops! You lost your keys. Miss your next turn.

Observing details

Lighting Strikes!

One of Benjamin Franklin's most famous experiments was the one in which he proved lightning was electricity. He used a kite and a key on the roof of his house to prove this. Look at the pictures below. The pictures in each row seem to look alike, but look again! Circle the picture that is different in each row.

Nouns
Noun Names

You may already know that a noun names a person, place or thing. A common noun names any person, place or thing. Examples of common nouns are *city, day* and *baby*. A proper noun names a certain person, place or thing. Examples of proper nouns are *Chicago, Tuesday* and *Emily*.

Read these sentences about Benjamin Franklin. Underline the common nouns you see. Circle the proper nouns.

1. Benjamin Franklin was a great inventor.

2. He lived in Philadelphia, Pennsylvania.

3. Ben studied lightning and electricity.

4. Franklin invented special eyeglasses.

5. The new glasses were called bifocals.

6. Benjamin invented a new stove.

7. Many people in America liked his stove.

8. The new stove had sliding doors.

9. The stoves that Ben made were smaller than old stoves.

10. They provided more heat than a fireplace.

11. Franklin sent reports of his work back to Britain.

12. Men in London gave Ben a special medal.

Practicing addition with regrouping
Franklin's Math

Did you know that Benjamin Franklin failed math as a young boy? His father took him out of school when he was only 10 years old so that he could help make candles and soap in the family's shop. In spite of this, Franklin went on to become a great inventor and scientist. Pretend that someone like Franklin, who didn't learn his math very well, completed this page. Can you find the errors?
Cross out every wrong answer you find. Write the correct answer below it.

1. $\begin{array}{r} 16 \\ + 13 \\ \hline 28 \end{array}$

2. $\begin{array}{r} 29 \\ + 13 \\ \hline 42 \end{array}$

3. $\begin{array}{r} 44 \\ + 39 \\ \hline 83 \end{array}$

4. $\begin{array}{r} 48 \\ + 43 \\ \hline 81 \end{array}$

5. $\begin{array}{r} 32 \\ + 32 \\ \hline 64 \end{array}$

6. $\begin{array}{r} 15 \\ + 17 \\ \hline 33 \end{array}$

7. $\begin{array}{r} 50 \\ + 18 \\ \hline 68 \end{array}$

8. $\begin{array}{r} 22 \\ + 38 \\ \hline 50 \end{array}$

9. $\begin{array}{r} 26 \\ + 15 \\ \hline 31 \end{array}$

10. $\begin{array}{r} 28 \\ + 21 \\ \hline 47 \end{array}$

11. $\begin{array}{r} 46 \\ + 32 \\ \hline 88 \end{array}$

12. $\begin{array}{r} 19 \\ + 16 \\ \hline 35 \end{array}$

13. $\begin{array}{r} 54 \\ + 37 \\ \hline 92 \end{array}$

14. $\begin{array}{r} 21 \\ + 64 \\ \hline 83 \end{array}$

15. $\begin{array}{r} 65 \\ + 25 \\ \hline 90 \end{array}$

16. $\begin{array}{r} 49 \\ + 31 \\ \hline 70 \end{array}$

Science information and experiments

Learning About Lightning

Your students' study of the life of Ben Franklin will lead to a natural curiosity about lightning–what it is, how it works and so on. The information and activities on these two pages will help you answer their questions and lead them to learn more about lightning and electricity.

Teacher Background Information

A lightning bolt is an enormous release of static electric charge. Usually, we experience only small amounts of static electricity when we take clothes from the dryer, brush our hair or walk across thick carpeting and then touch a metal doorknob. Most of the time the sparks from these static electric releases are not visible, so your students may not be able to readily make the connection between static electricity and lightning. Lead your students in Activity #1 on p. 54 to help increase their knowledge.

Understanding lightning requires some knowledge of positive and negative charges. As you may remember, electrons are tiny particles that circle the outside of atoms. They carry a negative charge. Positive ions are atoms or molecules that have lost an electron.

Normally atoms and molecules have equal positive and negative charges, making them neutral, but when different kinds of matter come in contact with each other, electrons are transferred. One of the materials gains extra electrons and becomes negatively charged. When an object carrying a lot of negative charges is placed close to an object with a positive charge, a spark jumps across the space between them to neutralize the charge.

During a thunderstorm, static electricity builds up between the Earth and the cloud and a spark in the form of an invisible lightning bolt comes down from the cloud. Just before this bolt reaches the ground, it is met with an upward moving, positively charged spark. When these two clash, an explosion occurs. The result is a visible flash of lightning.

You may want to tell your students that lightning is a common event around the world. At any given time there are about 2000 thunderstorms occurring around the Earth. A single bolt of lightning may be only a couple of inches wide, but it can move an astounding 90,000 miles per second! The power in the strike is 3,000,000 megawatts which compares to all the electricity generated in the U.S. at any one instant.

Of course, you will want to remind your students of safety rules to follow during thunderstorms. These include:

1. Stay inside away from large windows.
2. If you must be outside, seek a low ditch. Never stand under a tree.
3. Stay off the phone and away from plumbing. Lightning can strike above-ground phone and television cables and carry the charge into your home and appliances. Metal plumbing pipes are also good conductors and electricity.
4. Unplug televisions, computers (including phone lines) and microwaves. These items are easily damaged by lightning strikes.

Activity #1

Divide students into pairs and give each pair a piece of notebook paper, a piece of wool (mittens or pieces of an old sweater work well) and a flat piece of metal such as a pie pan or piece of foil. Darken the room as much as possible. Instruct one student in each pair to rub the wool on the paper, and then place the piece of metal on top of the paper. He should see a spark. (The rubbing puts a negative electrical charge on the paper. The metal sheet also carries a negative charge. This negative charge is increased when the metal is placed on the paper. When the students' fingers touch the metal the negative charge is attracted to the positive charge in their bodies and creates a spark.

Note: It often requires a lot of physical energy, i.e, rubbing, to produce enough of a charge to make a small, visible spark.) Partners may take turns.

Activity #2

Blow up a balloon. Draw a face on it with a permanent marker. Hang it from the ceiling with a string so that it is at about the same level as your students' heads. Ask a volunteer to rub the balloon with a piece of wool. Does the face on the balloon turn toward the person rubbing the balloon? Why? Ask the student to step away from the balloon, then move toward it. Allow other students to try the same procedure. Ask the class how close to the balloon they must be before the balloon face reacts. What do they think is happening?

Activity #3

Collect some Styrofoam™ packing pellets. Inflate a balloon and rub it with a wool cloth. Bring the balloon close to the pellets and watch what happens. Many of the pellets will cling to the balloon. Wait for several minutes and see what happens to the pellets. Try to explain the forces that were involved in the pellets being attracted, then explain that these forces (charges) change over time and the attraction is no longer there.

Search other books and the internet for more scientific experiments that help to explain static electricity and lightning.

Resources

These books are recommended for ages 4-8.

Ben Franklin and the Magic Squares (Step into Reading, Step 3) by Frank Murphy. Random House, 2001.

Discover Electricity by Rae Bains. Troll Communications, 1982.

The Hatmaker's Sign: A Story by Ben Franklin by Ben Franklin et al. Orchard Books, 2000.

Meet Benjamin Franklin by Maggie Scarf. Random House, 2002.

A Picture Book of Benjamin Franklin by David Adler, et al. Holiday House, 1991.

Where Does Electricity Come From? by C. Vance Cast. Barron's Educational Series, 1992.

Young Ben Franklin (Easy Biographies) by Laurence Santrey. Troll Communications, 1990.

These books are for older readers, ages 8-12:

Awesome Experiments in Electricity and Magnetism by Michael Anthony DiSpezio, Sterling Publishing Company, Inc., 2000.

Ben and Me: An Astonishing Life of Benjamin Franklin As Written by His Good Mouse Amos by Robert Lawson. Little, Brown, and Co., 1988.

The Ben Franklin Book of Easy and Incredible Science Experiments by the Franklin Institute. John Wiley and Sons, Inc., 1995.

Benjamin Franklin's Adventures with Electricity by Beverly Birch, et al. Barron's Educational Series, Inc., 1996.

Benjamin Franklin: Young Printer (Childhood of Famous Americans Series) by Augusta Stevenson. Simon & Schuster, 1983.

What's the Big Idea, Ben Franklin? by Jean Fritz. The Putnam Publishing Group, 1996.

National Puzzle Day

January 29 is National Puzzle Day. It's a great day to have fun and challenge your students' problem-solving abilities, all at the same time!

Begin by reproducing the puzzle book on pages 57-58. Fold the pages as directed, and put them together like this to form a booklet:

Encourage students to take the booklets home and complete the puzzles with their families. Many of the pages can be colored, too.

In addition to the other skill pages in this section, try some of these puzzling activities with your students during January:

• Work a jigsaw puzzle or two as a class. Leave one out on a large table so that several students may work on it together in their free time.

• Bring in manipulative puzzles and games such as a Rubik's™ cube, a Jenga™ game and others.

• Make your own classroom puzzles from old calendar pictures. First select six (or more) appropriate pictures. Then choose six different colors of construction paper. Make sure the colored pages are larger than the pictures. Glue each picture on a piece of construction paper so that a "frame" of color is formed around the picture. After the glue has dried completely, cut each picture into several pieces. (The number of pieces and the shapes that

you cut will depend on the age and ability of your students.) Place each puzzle in its own resealable plastic bag. Encourage students to try all of the puzzles. You don't need to worry about pieces getting mixed up because each puzzle has its own color on the back of every piece. And students can tell which pieces belong around the border of the puzzle because of the "frame" effect.

• Present "a puzzle a day" during puzzle week. Use brainteasers such as these:
  1. What can go up the chimney down but not down the chimney up? (umbrella)
  2. What keys are too big for your pocket? (donkeys, monkeys or turkeys)
  3. What is the longest sentence you can think of in which every word begins with B?
  4. What is a two-word rhyme for these? a. a dance for hogs   b. a nicer cardigan (pig jig, better sweater)
  5. Name at least five parts of the body that are spelled with three letters. (ear, eye, arm, leg, toe, rib, etc.)

Puzzle Book

See page 56 for instructions.

9

¿

How many words can you spell with the letters in your name? Write them here:

_____   _____

Write your first and last name.

Fold here first.

1

This book belongs to

Fold here second.

Start

Find a path to the star.

I am a "maze"ing!

My Puzzle Book

Finish drawing the snowman.

How many circles do you see?

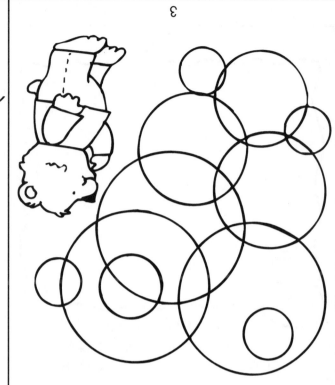

Fold here first.

Fold here second.

Find names of 9 animals
that are spelled with 3 letters.

D T A B P
C O W I F
A W G K O
T L S L X
Y E N E H

bat   cat   cow
dog   elk   hen
fox   owl   pig

5

Circle the two snowflakes
that are the same.

2

58

Name _____

Even and odd numbers
Winter Dot-to-Dot

A dot-to-dot is a special kind of puzzle. You won't know what the picture is until you connect the dots! On this page you need to connect only the dots that have even numbers. Connect them in order beginning with 2 and 4.

TLC10408 Copyright © Teaching & Learning Company, Carthage, IL 62321-0010

Name _____

Spelling Riddle

What do you call a cow on a roller coaster? If you follow the directions carefully on this page, you will spell the answer. Think about how the word for each picture below is spelled. Find the special letter in each line. The first one is done for you.

1. the letter that's in but not in    <u>M</u>

2. the letter that's in but not in   ____

3. the letter that's in but not in   ____

4. the letter that's in but not in   ____

5. the letter that's in but not in   ____

6. the letter that's in but not in   ____

7. the letter that's in but not in   ____

8. the letter that's in but not in   ____

9. the letter that's in  but not in    ____

Now read the word going down this page, and you will know what to call a cow on a roller coaster!

Name _____

Animal Riddles

Can you solve each animal riddle on this page? Read all the clues carefully.
Then write your answer in each blank.

1.

I live on a farm.
I have four legs.
I am covered with soft wool.

What am I?

_____

2.

I do not have a backbone.
I live in the ground.
Sometimes I come out of the
   ground after it rains.
I'm Squishy and slimey.

What am I?

_____

3.

I live in the water.
I have a backbone.
I am covered with scales.

What am I?

_____

4.

I have two legs.
My body is covered with
   feathers.
My babies are called chicks.

What am I?

_____

5.

I have four legs.
I am a reptile.
I can hide inside my shell.

What am I?

_____

6.

I use my wings to fly.
I come out of a cocoon.
I can be very colorful.

What am I?

_____

Writing equations
Puzzling Math

Can you find secret math sentences in each line below? Remember what you know about addition, subtraction, multiplication and division. Then circle numbers in each row that make a math fact. Write each fact as a number sentence in the lines provided. Do not change the order of the numbers. There are extra numbers in some rows.

Example: 0   15   6   9   7   4   10   14

$15 - 6 = 9$ $4 + 10 = 14$

1.   4   6   24   5   9   2   11   6

_____

2.   12   4   3   6   18   2   9   5

_____

3.   13   9   4   2   8   5   13   2

_____

4.   7   6   42   10   32   8   4   2

_____

5.   10   2   5   5   0   3   9   27

_____

6.   8   1   8   2   16   4   4   1

_____

7.   9   11   2   22   10   12   6   2

Bookmarks

Use these bookmarks during the special days in January.

Award Certificates

This award goes to

_____

This person has been stirring up some great work during Oatmeal Month.

Presented by

_____

on

_____

Congratulations!

A special award goes to

_____

for starting the New Year with excellent behavior.

Keep up the good work!

_____
Teacher

_____
Date

This

Ben Franklin Award

is hereby presented to

_____

for excellent work and citizenship.

Congratulations!

Keep up the electrifying performance!

Presented on

_____

By

February

Get ready for a fabulous February with all the great helps in this book! Here is a fresh assortment of bulletin boards, teacher helps, and curriculum reproducible pages to see you through many of the special days in February.

We've chosen six special themes for this month: Black History Month, Groundhog Day, Thomas Edison's birthday, Valentine's Day, Presidents' Day and Pancake Day. For some of these themes you will find bulletin boards and resource lists. For others you might see a song, a student game idea or an art idea. For all of the units you will have appealing reproducibles that cover important primary level skills. Most skill sheets are for math or language, but we've also included some pages for science, social studies and general thinking skills.

Simply pick the themes you are most interested in and select activities and worksheets that are on an appropriate level for your students. You will be able to use many ideas in each unit even though some individual pages may be too difficult or too simple for your particular class.

First your students will learn about important African Americans of the past. Rosa Parks, Harriet Tubman and Jim Thorpe are some of the featured Americans. A resource list (located after the language and math pages) includes many interesting books for early readers.

Groundhogs are the feature of the second section. Students will learn about groundhog burrows, play a game, sing a song and work on reading and math skills as well.

In the Thomas Edison section you will find a bulletin board idea, and students will work with a time line, a graph and more.

Valentine's Day and Presidents' Day are, of course, included in this section. There are Valentine tongue twisters and a presidential mural idea in addition to several reading, writing and math skill pages.

The final section features pancakes. We've included some basic recipes and fun reproducibles for you and your students.

Don't miss the last three pages of this section that show an all-month bulletin board idea, bookmarks and award certificates. These pages may be used anytime throughout the month. And don't forget all the great bonus clip art on the CD. It promises to create a truly fabulous February for your students!

Name _____

Teacher: February is Black History Month. It's a great time to enjoy music performed and recorded by popular African Americans—both past and present.

Identifying musical instruments

Musicians

We can be thankful for many outstanding African American musicians.
Louie Armstrong, Marian Anderson, Diana Ross and Stevie Wonder are just a few.
Look at the objects in each row below. Cross out the one that is not used to make music.

On the back of this page, draw a picture of the
musical instrument that you would like to play.

Name _____

Musical Match

Mrs. Jackman's class is practicing music for a Black History Month celebration.
Look at all the instruments she has! There are two of almost every kind of instrument.
Draw a line to connect each instrument to a matching one.
When you are finished, you should have one instrument left over. Color that one.

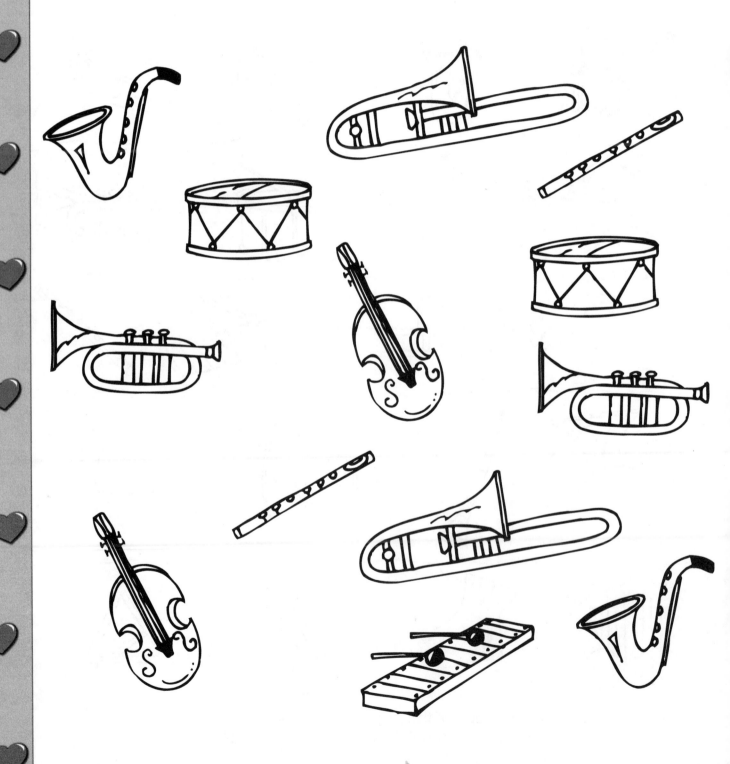

TLC10408 Copyright © Teaching & Learning Company, Carthage, IL 62321-0010

Name _____

Contractions
Harriet and Rosa

A contraction is one word made by putting two words together. One or more letters are left out. An apostrophe (') takes the place of the missing letter or letters.

For example: is not = isn't

Read each sentence below that tells about either Harriet Tubman or Rosa Parks. Circle the contraction in each one. Write the two words that mean the same as the contraction in the blanks. Choose from the words in the box below.

could not	was not	will not	they are	he is
should not	she is	would not	did not	let us

1. Harriet Tubman wasn't shy about helping others. _____

2. She didn't let her fear of being caught stop her. _____

3. Once Harriet escaped she couldn't stand the idea of leaving her family behind.

_____

4. Rosa Parks wouldn't agree with African Americans being forced to sit in the back of the bus.

_____

5. One day she told herself, "I won't sit at the back today." _____

6. And she didn't. She sat in the front and was arrested. _____

7. Other African Americans decided, "She's right!" _____

8. They said, "Let's not ride any bus until the laws are changed."

_____

The African Americans of Montgomery, Alabama, refused to ride buses in their city for one year. That meant long, tiring walks. But when the laws were finally changed, they knew the boycott was worth it!

Name _____

Harriet Tubman

Do you know about the life of Harriet Tubman? You may know that she was an African American woman who escaped from slavery and then helped many others escape, too. Learn more about her as you complete this activity.

Read the sentence beginnings on the left.
Match each one to the correct sentence ending on the right.

_____ 1. Harriet found out

_____ 2. She ran away by using

_____ 3. The underground railroad

_____ 4. People against slavery

_____ 5. They had hiding places in their homes,

_____ 6. Everyone who helped the slaves

_____ 7. After Harriet escaped,

_____ 8. In all, Harriet made more than 20 trips

A. and they planned routes through rivers, streams and roadways.

B. was not a real railroad.

C. risked their own lives.

D. and helped over 300 slaves escape.

E. that she was going to be sold.

F. the underground railroad.

G. she went back to help her family escape.

H. worked together to set up a system of escape routes.

Name _____

Searching for Heroes

Listed here are the names of many important African Americans. Can you find each name in the word search? Look for the part of the name that is in CAPITALS. Cross out each name as you find it. Names may appear up and down, across or diagonally, both backwards and forwards.

Muhammad ALI (boxer)
Marian ANDERSON (singer)
Louis ARMSTRONG (musician)
Benjamin BANNEKER (surveyor)
Romare BEARDEN (artist)
Harry BELAFONTE (actor)
George Washington CARVER (educator)
Bill COSBY (entertainer)
Marion JONES (athlete)
Michael JORDAN (basketball star)
Martin Luther KING, Jr. (civil rights leader)
Thurgood MARSHALL (Supreme Court justice)
Garrett A. MORGAN (inventor)
Jesse OWENS (athlete)
Rosa PARKS (civil rights activist)
Jackie ROBINSON (baseball star)
Harriet TUBMAN (underground railroad conductor)
Booker T. WASHINGTON (educator)

W	N	X	L	N	A	M	B	U	T	Z	A
Y	A	V	L	C	A	R	V	E	R	Q	R
R	D	S	A	A	Y	Z	T	N	A	N	M
E	R	E	H	B	L	N	K	O	N	E	S
K	O	N	S	I	O	I	W	S	D	D	T
E	J	O	R	F	N	E	Q	N	E	R	R
N	C	J	A	G	N	G	X	I	R	A	O
N	W	L	M	S	V	Y	T	B	S	E	N
A	E	X	P	A	R	K	S	O	O	B	G
B	Z	N	A	G	R	O	M	R	N	V	X

Name _____

Help Harriet

Pretend that Harriet Tubman is planning to help some slaves escape to freedom. Look at the maze below. With a red crayon, mark a path where she can pick up exactly 10 people. Then with a blue crayon, draw a different route where she can help 12 people.

Name _____

Solving word problems using addition and subtraction
Ages and Stages

Learn more about important African Americans as you solve the word problems on this page. For some problems you will need to add. For others you will need to subtract. Sometimes you will need to use information in an earlier question to find your answers. Read carefully and double check your math!

1. Jim Thorpe has been called "the Greatest American Athlete of the First Half of the Twentieth Century." He was born in 1888, and in 1912 he won Olympic gold medals for the pentathlon and decathlon. How old was Jim when he won the medals?

2. Jim Thorpe played both professional football and baseball. He played professional baseball from 1913 to 1919. How many years did he play pro baseball?

3. Jim Thorpe played professional football from 1917-1929. How old was Jim when he quit playing professional football?

4. Jackie Robinson was an outstanding athlete, businessman and civil rights leader. He was born in 1919. He began his professional baseball career in 1945. How old was he when he started playing professional baseball?

5. Jackie Robinson became the first African American to play major league baseball in the 20th century on April 15, 1947. Twelve years later all the major league teams had at least one African American ball player. What year was that?

6. In 1962, Robinson became the first African American to be named to the National Baseball Hall of Fame. How old was he then?

7. Wilma Rudolph was the first African American woman to win three track-and-field events at one Olympic Games. She was born in 1940. Because of polio, she could not walk normally until she was 11. What year was that?

8. Wilma won medals at the 1960 Olympic Games for the 100-meter, 200-meter and for running the last leg of the 4 x 100-meter relay team. Then she retired from running and became a teacher. She died at the age of 54. In what year did Wilma die?

Collage

A collage is a picture made from little bits of other pictures or objects. Romare Bearden was the African American artist who was known for his masterful collages. Make your own collage by following these directions:

1. Choose an animal or a favorite object as the theme of your collage.

2. Start with a sheet of white paper. Draw a simple sketch of your object.

3. Use scrap paper, construction paper, tissue paper and colored pictures from magazines and catalogs. Choose scraps and pictures with the colors you want to use for your collage.

4. Tear these colored papers into small pieces.

5. Lay the pieces on one section of the drawing. Overlap them to mix the colors.

6. Brush liquid starch or liquid glue over the colored paper scraps. The colors will run to create a wet-wash effect.

7. Repeat steps 5 and 6 until your drawing is completely covered. Let the collage dry overnight.

8. Use markers to draw details to your collage, if you desire.

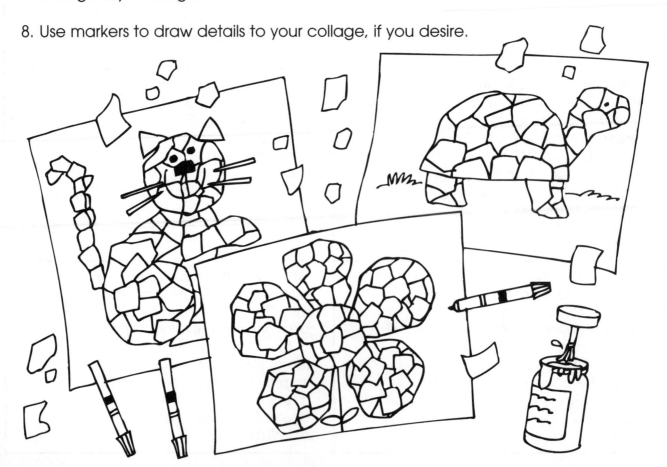

Resources

Celebrate the many important contributions African Americans have made to our world by choosing some of these books to read aloud to your students. Most are biographies for ages 4-8.

Duke Ellington: The Piano Prince and His Orchestra (Caldecott Honor Book) by Andrea Davis Pinkney, Disney Press, April 1998.

George Washington Carver: A Photo-Illustrated Biography (Read and Discover Photo-Illustrated Biographies) by Margo McLoone. Bridgestone Books, 1997.

Harriet and the Promised Land by Jacob Lawrence, Aladdin Paperbacks, 1997.

If I Only Had a Horn : Young Louis Armstrong by Roxane Orgill. Houghton Mifflin Co., 1997.

Jesse Owens (On My Own Biography) by Jane Sutcliffe. Lerner Pub Group, 2000.

Martin's Big Words: The Life of Dr. Martin Luther King, Jr., by Doreen Rappaport. Jump at the Sun, 2001.

Me and Uncle Romie: A Story Inspired by the Life and Art of Romare Bearden by Claire Hartfield, et al. Dial Books for Young Readers, December 2002.

A Picture Book of Rosa Parks (Picture Book Biography) by David A. Adler, Holiday House, Reprint edition, 1995.

Tiger Woods (Real-Life Reader Biography) by John Albert Torres. Mitchell Lane Publishers, Inc., 2001.

When Marian Sang: The True Recital of Marian Anderson: The Voice of a Century by Pam Munoz Ryan, Scholastic Trade, 2002.

Wilma Rudolph (On My Own Biographies) by Victoria Sharrow, Carolrhoda Books, 2000.

Groundhog Day

According to popular tradition, on February 2, the groundhog, or woodchuck, comes out of his hole after winter hibernation to look for his shadow. If he sees his shadow, the forecast is for six more weeks of bad weather. If he cannot see his shadow, that means that spring is coming soon. Not surprisingly, statistical evidence does not support this tradtion. But this is a fun day to celebrate with your students, and a good time to talk about animals, hibernation and weather.

• Talk about animals that hibernate. Together look up information about groundhogs, bears and gophers. Find out where these animals live and what their burrows are like.

  Read the article on page 79 to learn more.

• Brainstorm to list as many words as possible to describe the weather. On the board write words such as *windy, sunny, rainy* and so on. Ask each student to draw a picture that shows one of these weather words. Post pictures together on a classroom wall to make a weather mural.

• Just before Groundhog Day, ask students to predict whether or not the groundhog will see his shadow. Together make a bar graph to show the number of yes and no votes. Then watch the weather closely on February 2, and listen to news accounts of the weather at the official groundhog's home. (Punxsutawney Phil lives in Pennsylvania.)

Instructions for Groundhog Day Matchup on page 77:

Before Playing: Photocopy the game cards on page 77. If you like, color and laminate them. Cut the cards apart. Select two students to play the game together.

To play, place the cards facedown on a table, and mix them up. Arrange them in rows and columns. Decide who plays first.

Player 1 chooses two cards and turns them faceup. If the cards match, the player keeps those cards and takes another turn. If the cards do not match, player 1 turns them facedown again in their same positions. Player 2 then takes a turn.

The game continues until there are no matches left. Players count the number of cards they earned during the game. The winner is the one with the most cards.

Groundhog Day Matchup

See page 76 for instructions for this two-player game.

TLC10408 Copyright © Teaching & Learning Company, Carthage, IL 62321-0010

A Song for Groundhog Day

Here's a good action song to sing on February 2.
You may want to take students to the gym or playground for this one.

Did You Ever See a Groundhog?

To the tune of "Did You Ever See a Lassie?"

Did you ever see a groundhog,   (Hold hands up to eyes as if they were binoculars.)
A groundhog, a groundhog,
Did you ever see a groundhog
Go hide in the ground?   (Run a few steps and crouch down to the floor.)
Go hide in the ground,
Go hide in the ground,
Did you ever see a groundhog
Go hide in the ground?

Did you ever see a groundhog,   (Hold hands up to eyes as if they were binoculars.)
A groundhog, a groundhog,
Did you ever see a groundhog
Come peeking outside?   (Stand on tiptoes and peer around the room.)
Come peeking outside,
Come peeking outside,
Did you ever see a groundhog
Come peeking outside?

Did you ever see a groundhog,   (Hold hands up to eyes as if they were binoculars.)
A groundhog, a groundhog,
Did you ever see a groundhog
Discover his shadow?   (Look surprised and pleased.)
Discover his shadow,
Discover his shadow,
Did you ever see a groundhog
Discover his shadow?

Yes, I've always seen a groundhog,   (Nod head up and down.)
A groundhog, a groundhog,
Yes, I've always seen a groundhog
Run this way and that.   (Run around the room.)
Run this way and that way,
Run this way and that way,
Yes, I've always seen a groundhog
Run this way and that.

Name _____

Where Are You, Mr. Groundhog?

Read this article about groundhogs. Then answer the questions below.

Groundhogs, as well as other animals such as gophers, prairie dogs and field mice, dig their own homes under the ground. Their homes are called burrows. The groundhogs make sleeping rooms, food storage rooms and connecting tunnels. They even plan emergency exits in case one escape route is blocked.

Most groundhogs first dig their burrows in September or October when the weather turns colder. Many of them stay there until warmer temperatures arrive in March. That means the groundhogs live almost six months underground in their cozy burrows. It's no wonder that they work so hard to make nice underground homes!

For each item, circle all the correct answers.

1. This article was mostly about:
   a. the groundhog and his shadow
   b. underground homes
   c. Groundhog Day

2. Why do groundhogs spend almost six months underground?
   a. cold weather
   b. they are afraid of people
   c. that's where they eat

3. What do groundhogs build in their underground homes?
   a. rooms for storing food
   b. rooms for sleeping
   c. escape routes

4. Do you think groundhogs are comfortable in their burrows? Why?

5. On the back of this page, draw a picture of a gopher's underground home.

Solving a maze

Let's Go Burrowing!

Mr. Groundhog is trying to get out of his burrow to learn if he can see his shadow. His usual path out of his home has been blocked. Luckily, he built another exit. Can you help him find it? Draw a line with your crayon to show Mr. Groundhog how he can get out.

TLC10408 Copyright © Teaching & Learning Company, Carthage, IL 62321-0010

Name _____

Compound words
Compound Animals

The name of the groundhog is a compound word. It is made from the two words *ground* and *hog*. How do you think this animal came to be named this way?

There are several other animals that have compound words for their names. See if you can figure out nine of them by matching the first part of the animal name to the correct second part. Draw a line to connect the right parts. Note: Some names are spelled with one word. Some are spelled with two words.

Write the animal names here:

1. bob	eater	1. _____
2. sea	pig	2. _____
3. rattle	crab	3. _____
4. guinea	cat	4. _____
5. gold	deer	5. _____
6. ant	horse	6. _____
7. dragon	snake	7. _____
8. rein	fish	8. _____
9. sand	fly	9. _____

Draw and color a picture of one of the animal names you wrote.

Addition and subtraction using a code
Groundhog Math

These little groundhogs are doing their math lesson. But they don't use numbers! They use the pictures shown here. Find out the answer to each problem by using the chart. Then write your answer, with both a picture and a number.

Chart
1 = ♡
2 = ☀
3 = ◆
4 = ☾
5 = □
6 = ☺
7 = ⇦
8 = ▲
9 = ✿

1. ◆ + ☀ =

2. ▲ - ♡ =

3. □ + ☾ =

4. ✿ - ♡ =

5. ☺ + ☀ =

6. ⇦ - ☺ =

7. ☀ + ⇦ =

8. ✿ - □ =

9. ☾ + ♡ =

10. ▲ - ◆ =

Now make up your own pictures for the numbers 11 and 12. Use them to write two new math problems. Give the problems to a friend to solve.

11 =

12 =

1.

2.

Name _____

Feet Feat

One groundhog has four feet. Two groundhogs have eight feet. Finish filling out the numbers under the pictures to show how many feet are in each group of groundhogs.

__4__ feet	__8__ feet	_____ feet
_____ feet	_____ feet	_____ feet
_____ feet	_____ feet	_____ feet

TLC10408 Copyright © Teaching & Learning Company, Carthage, IL 62321-0010

Thomas Edison's Birthday

America's most famous inventor, Thomas Alva Edison, was born on February 11, 1847. His birthday is now widely observed as Inventor's Day. Edison was born in Milan, Ohio, and he died at Menlo Park, New Jersey, in 1931. He held 1093 patents—the most ever issued to a single person. Edison said that "genius is one percent inspiration and ninety-nine percent perspiration." His persistence led to great accomplishments including electric lighting, the phonograph, moving pictures and improvements to the telephone and telegraph.

Edison's greatest invention was, perhaps, the incandescent light bulb. The shape book on page 85, the bulletin board on page 86, and the following activities deal with light:

• Talk with your students about different sources of light. Brainstorm together and write your list on the board. Ideas include: the sun, light bulbs, flashlights, stars, fireworks, candles and so on.

• Talk about the brightness of light. (See page 90 for an activity about wattages of bulbs.) Show students that the farther you are from a light the less bright it seems. Do this by shining a flashlight on a wall. Watch the pool of light grow larger and dimmer as you move the flashlight away. Explain that light spreads out in all directions from its source. So when you are far away, the light is spread over a wide area. Tell students that many stars, for example, are much brighter than our sun, but their light is spread out over so large an area that by the time it reaches us, it seems very dim.

• Bring in a lamp that uses an ordinary electric light bulb, and one that uses a fluorescent light bulb. Leave both lamps on for several minutes. Then ask students to come near the lamps and place their hands above each one. Do they notice that the electric bulb produces heat, but the fluorescent bulb does not? Tell students that fluorescent bulbs contain different gases than electric bulbs and produce light in a different way. Help them to learn that fluorescent bulbs waste less energy and are more economical to use.

• Did you know that some fish give out light? In the very dark deep-sea areas, the only light is produced by the fish themselves. Some glow because of a coating of luminous "slime." Others have luminous bacteria on their bodies. Find information on these fish to share with your learners. Examples of luminous fish include lantern fish, lamp-eye fish, and anglerfish.

Be sure to check out some of the resources on page 94. Curious students may enjoy learning about all sorts of inventions. All are certain to enjoy hearing you read to them a biography of Thomas Edison, America's greatest inventor.

Shape Book Pattern

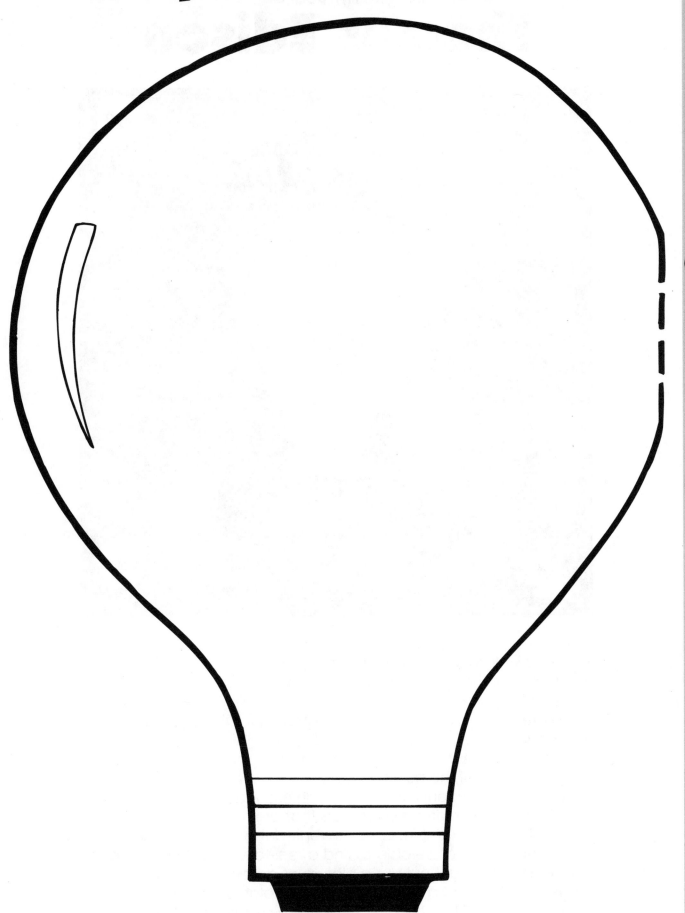

Thomas Edison

- Use dark blue or black background paper.
- Cut out a large yellow light bulb to use in the center of the display.
- Use green, red, white or light blue lettering for the board's title.
- Ask each student to cut out a small light bulb using a pattern from page 87. He should write his name on the front and add it to the border of the bulletin board.
- Next, instruct students to look through magazines, catalogs and newspapers for pictures of objects that are related to Edison's inventions. For example, Edison invented the motion picture, but students might not be able to find a reel-to-reel movie projector. Instead, they might cut out a picture of a video. Or they might select a picture of a CD player which is related to the phonograph invented by Edison. Add all these pictures to the display.

TLC10408 Copyright © Teaching & Learning Company, Carthage, IL 62321-0010

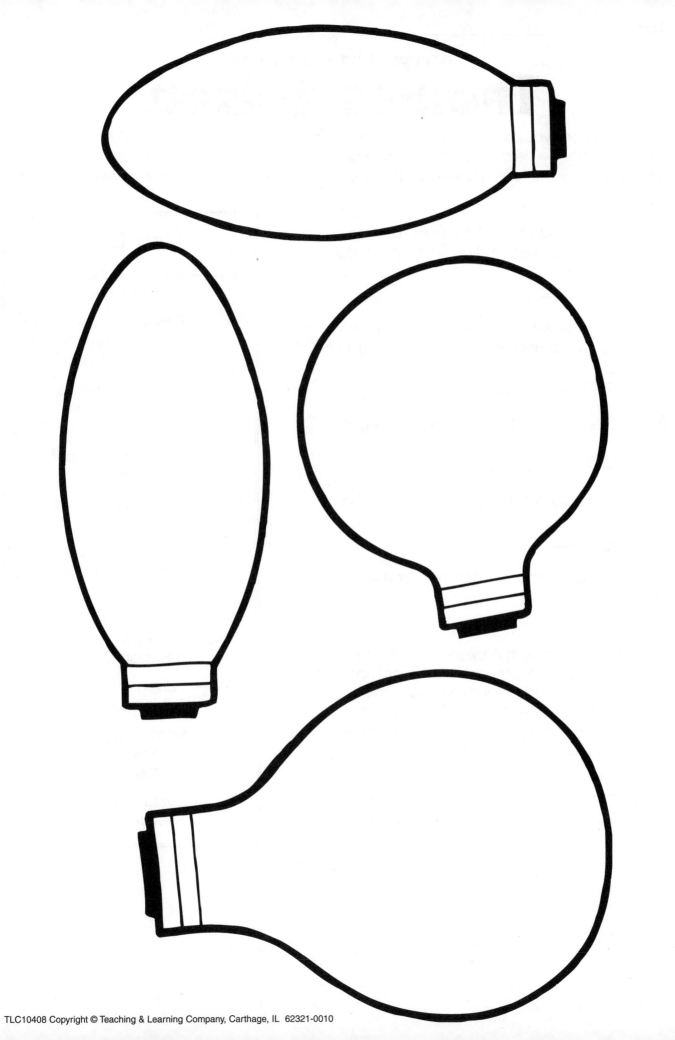

Name _____

Interpreting a time line

Thomas Edison

Thomas Edison was probably the most important inventor in the history of America. Did you know that he held patents, or legal rights, to more that 1000 inventions? Study the time line below the learn more about some of his inventions. Then answer the questions.

1. Edison worked on the light bulb for many long years. In what year did he finally get it right?

   _____

2. How long was it after the time Edison perfected the light bulb until he began the world's first

   power station? _____

3. Did Edison live in the same state during his

   entire life? _____

4. Which came first, the phonograph or the

   movies? _____

5. Which came first, the light bulb or the voting

   machine? _____

6. Edison worked with Alexander Graham Bell on the telephone. Bell received the patent, but Edison improved Bell's design to make a person's voice louder and clearer. Bell received a patent on the telephone in 1876. What else happened in that year for Edison?

   _____

7. How old was Edison when he died?

   _____

Time Line

1847 — Thomas Edison was born in Milan, Ohio.

1869 — Edison was awarded his first patent. It was for a voting machine.

1876 — Edison opened a laboratory at Menlo Park, New Jersey.

1877 — Edison invented the phonograph.

1879 — Edison perfected the electric light bulb.

1882 — Edison started the world's first power station.

1889 — Edison started the General Electric company.

1893 — Edison invented the first motion picture.

1900 — Edison invented alkaline storage batteries.

1931 — Edison died in New Jersey.

88

Name _____

Bar graph master
Let's Vote!

Think about some of Edison's most famous inventions: the light bulb, the battery, motion pictures and phonographs. (Ask your teacher to explain any of these to you that you do not understand.) Talk with your classmates about which one of these you think is most important. Then vote for your favorite.

Keep track of all the votes of your classmates. Write tally marks in the spaces below.

Invention	Votes
Light bulb	
Battery	
Motion pictures	
Phonograph	

Raise your hand to vote for...

Now put your information into this bar graph.
Draw a bar for each invention to show how many votes there were for that item.

Light bulb																		
Battery																		
Motion pictures																		
Phonograph																		
	1	2	3	4	5	6	7	8	9	10	11	12	13	14	15	16	17	18

Name _____

Ranking numbers
What Watt?

Did you know that not all light bulbs make the same amount of light? All light bulbs have a number that tells how many watts they produce. Watts are units that measure electrical power. Light bulbs with lower watts make less light than bulbs with higher watts. Pretend that the smallest light bulb here makes the least light, and that the largest makes the most light, and so on. Cut out the watt numbers from the bottom of the page. Arrange them in order from the lowest to the highest.
Then paste the lowest number under the smallest light bulb, the second lowest number under the second smallest light bulb and so on.

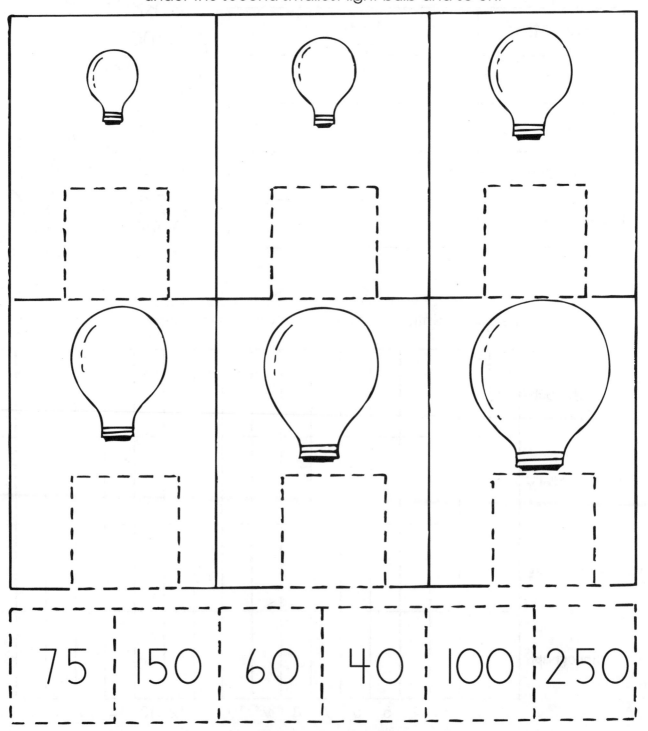

Name _____

Inventor at Work

Some of Edison's inventions were quick to make. Others took years and years.
Often we have to try many new things before we find something that works.
Imagine that a young girl named Emily is trying to invent a new gadget to tie shoelaces.
Read the steps she might go through. Number them in order from 1 to 9.

_____ Emily tries to put strings through paper clips.

_____ Emily puts the paper clips and rubber bands away and gets out twisties.

_____ Emily thinks there must be an easier way to tie shoes.

_____ She snaps the rubber bands, and the paper clips fall off.

_____ Emily discovers the twisties won't work.

_____ Emily connects the paper clips to rubber bands.

_____ Emily puts the twisties away and decides to try again tomorrow.

_____ Emily decides to try to make a new machine to tie shoestrings.

_____ She tries to hold shoelaces together with the twisties.

Name _____

Plurals
Many Inventions!

Thomas Edison invented over 1000 new things. Many, many other inventors through history have invented many more. Listed below are some interesting inventions. Next to each word, write the correct word that means "more than one."

Remember:
- Add *-s* to most nouns: car—cars, book—books
- Add *-es* to nouns that end in *s, ss, ch* or *x*: buses, dresses, churches, foxes

1. zipper _____

2. eyeglass _____

3. paper _____

4. watch _____

5. pencil _____

6. wrench _____

7. toaster _____

8. rocket _____

9. cardboard box _____

10. wheel _____

11. light switch _____

12. button _____

13. compass _____

14. sandwich _____

15. airplane _____

16. computer _____

17. match _____

18. ruler _____

Draw a picture of one of the inventions listed above.

Name _____

Inventive Sentences

Think about something you would like to invent.
Then finish each sentence with your own words. Remember to use punctuation.

1. I would like to invent _____

   because _____

2. I would need to use _____

3. If I needed help, I could ask _____

4. It would be fun to try _____

5. I wonder if _____

6. People who would like to use my invention are _____

   _____

7. I could sell my invention at _____

8. My ad for this invention would say _____

9. A different idea for an invention is _____

10. The way to become an inventor is _____

   _____

   _____

On the back, draw a magazine ad for one of your invention ideas.

Resources

Books

Imaginative Inventions: The Who, What, Where, When, and Why of Roller Skates, Potato Chips, Marbles, and Pie (and More!) by Charice Mericle Harper. Little Brown Children's Books, 2001. For ages 5-8

I Wonder Why Zippers Have Teeth: And Other Questions About Inventions by Barbara Taylor. Kingfisher, 1996. For ages 5-8

Perseverance! The Story of Thomas Alva Edison by Peter Murray. The Child's World, Inc. , 1997. For ages 7 -11.

A Picture Book of Thomas Alva Edison by David Adler, Holiday House, Inc., 1999.

The Science of a Light Bulb by Neville Evans. Raintree Publishers, 2000. For ages 7-9.

The Story of Thomas Alva Edison, Inventor: The Wizard of Menlo Park by Margaret Davidson. Scholastic, Inc., 1990. For ages 7-10.

Switch On, Switch Off by Melvin Berger. HarperCollins Children's Books, 1990. For ages 5-9.

Thomas Edison by Ann Gaines. Rourke Publishing, LLC, 2002. For ages 6-9.

The Thomas Edison Book of Easy and Incredible Experiments by James G. Cook, Thomas Alva Foundation Edison (Contributor). John Wiley & Sons, 1988. For ages 9-12.

Thomas Edison: Inventor by Carin T. Ford, Enslow Publishers, 2002. For ages 6-9.

Toys! Amazing Stories Behind Some Great Inventions by Don L. Wulffson. Henry Holt & Company, Inc., 2000. For ages 8-12.

Young Tom Edison: Great Inventor by Claire Nemes (Editor), Troll Communications, 1995. For ages 5-7.

VHS and DVD

Edison: The Wizard of Light, Steeplechase Video, March 2001. (UPC: 699359100525)

94

Valentine's Day

The next two pages are filled with fun and worthwhile Valentine ideas for your class. Choose the ones that will work best for you.

Tongue Twisters

Start the Valentine season with one of these fun tongue twisters:

> Sally sends Sal a silly song.
> Lovesick Lloyd loves Lulu's lollipops.
> Cupid's capers carried Carrie.

Here are some ideas for using these and other tongue twisters:

• First, be sure the students know the meanings of all the words. *Capers* are "playful jumps" or "playful activities" according to one dictionary.

• Then ask students to try saying one tongue twister at a time altogether. Do this several times until students can master all the words.

• Next, ask if any student wants to try to say the twister as fast as he can all by himself. Be ready for some laughs, and try to be sure that no one feels embarrassed if he stumbles. Courage should be applauded!

• Also, you may want to use the twisters for handwriting lessons. Each of these twisters emphasis one letter of the alphabet. For example, if your students need practice writing an uppercase *S*, ask them to copy the first tongue twister several times in their best handwriting. Write other tongue twisters of your own for other letters.

• Another Idea: Ask students to write one of the twisters at the bottom of a large sheet of blank paper. Then instruct them to illustrate it with markers or crayons.

Poetry

Here are some Valentine poems your students might enjoy:

Roses are red,
Violets are blue,
Orchids are pink,
And I love you!

Love is kind,
Love is caring,
Love is what
I am sharing.

It's February fourteenth
And I'd just like to say
I wish you a happy
Saint Valentine's Day!

Here are some suggestions for using these poems:

Choral Reading: Divide students into three groups. Let each group practice reciting one of the poems together to present to the whole class.

Valentines: Students may copy one of these poems into a handmade Valentine card.

Pattern Writing: Students can use the pattern in one of the poems to write their own original verse. For example, a child might write: Love is warm, love is nice . . . Another might write: Love is safe, Love is true . . .

Valentine Cards

Here are brief instructions for cute Valentine cards your students can make.

Sewing Valentine: Cut a large heart out of red or pink poster board. Use a hole punch to make holes along the edge of the heart. (Holes should be about ¹/₂" apart and about ¹/₂" from the outer edge.) Use a blunt plastic needle to sew white yarn through the holes. Write *I love you SEW much!* on the heart.

Chewing Gum Valentine: Ask students to cut a large heart out of any appropriate color of heavy paper. Then tell them to write *Won't CHEW be my Valentine?* on the heart. Finally, tape a wrapped piece of sugarless chewing gum to each card.

Secret Message Valentine: Write a Valentine message using a secret code. Here is a code you can use: A = 1, B = 2, C = 3, D = 4 . . . Z = 26. First write the message you want to send on a piece of scrap paper. Then write it again onto a card, substituting a number for each letter of the message. As an example, ask your students to decode this message:

9   12- 15- 22- 5   25- 15- 21!

Remind students to enclose a copy of the code with the secret-message valentine. (See page 105 for a Valentine riddle in a different code.)

Valentine's Day

Get ready for Valentine's Day with this bulletin board. Every student can add his own touch!

Use a white background with black or red letters for the title. Add a tree, grass, sun or other basic outdoor scenery. Then let students do the rest! Here are two ideas:

1. Ask students to cut out several small hearts of various sizes. Then let them create their own brand-new animals made only of hearts. Add these animals to bulletin board—on the ground, in the tree or in the sky.

2. Ask students to write the name of their pet or their favorite animal on a heart and add it anywhere on the display. Suggest they make heart flowers, heart birds or heart leaves on the tree.

98

Name _____

Rhyming words
Heart Beat

What words rhyme with *heart* ? You might begin with *start*.
Say the name for each picture below. If the word rhymes with *heart,* color the picture.

Name _____

Correct the Consonants

Name each picture. Look at the word below it. One consonant is wrong. Draw a line through it. Write the correct consonant. The first one has been done for you.

hear~~s~~
t

bop

pace

rock

dot

leap

spar

ast

cand

Name _____

Heart Smart

Circle the direction that goes with each picture.

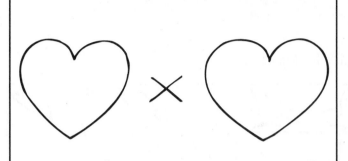

Put an X in the first heart.

Put an X in between the hearts.

Put an X in the second heart.

Underline the first heart.

Underline the second heart.

Cross out the first heart.

Put an A in the first heart and a Z in the second heart.

Put an A in the first heart and an X in the third heart.

Put an A in the first heart and a Z in the third heart.

Put a small heart in the first heart and a + in the last heart.

Put a small heart in the second heart and a + in the last heart.

Put a small heart in the second heart and a - in the last heart.

Put a small heart in the first heart and a smiley face in the last heart.

Put a small heart in the second heart and a smiley face in the last heart.

Put a small heart in the first heart and a star in the last heart.

Name _____

Action verbs
Valentine Action

Look at the picture of the Valentine's Day party. Everyone is busy!
A verb is an action word. It tells what is happening.

Patsy **hangs** balloons.

The word **hangs** is a verb. It tells what Patsy is doing.

Read each sentence. Circle the verb that tells what is happening.

1. Mrs. Cole makes punch.

2. Everyone gives cards to each other.

3. Ryan greets the visitors.

4. The parents eat the cookies.

5. Sheila helps her teacher serve the food.

6. At the end of the party, Mr. Rich tells stories.

TLC10408 Copyright © Teaching & Learning Company, Carthage, IL 62321-0010

Name _____

Story writing
Get Started!

Stories have a beginning, a middle and an end.
Write a beginning sentence for each Valentine story.

Example: <u>Stacy made three valentines.</u>
            She gave one to her friend, Laura.
            She gave the other two to her mom and dad.

1. _____

   He thanked Mrs. Smith for inviting him to the party.
   He walked home, carrying lots of cards and candy.

2. _____

   I hid them and kept them a secret until February 14.
   On Valentine's Day, my brother and sister were so surprised!

3. _____

   Spot raced to the kitchen to help lick up the mess.
   I guess he likes Valentine's Day, too.

4. _____

   It was so nice to hear Grandma's voice.
   I wished her a Happy Valentine's Day, too.

5. _____

   The two boys looked through a lot of cookbooks.
   They finally found a treat to make.

6. _____

   He wondered who could have sent it.
   He opened the card and saw it was from Uncle Bill.

Counting by fives
Cupid's Counting

Help Cupid deliver his message to Elisa. Count by fives from 5 to 100.
Color the squares with these numbers to show the path.

5	6	13	18	11	17	42
3	10	18	30	35	38	32
8	15	20	25	26	40	41
12	24	55	50	45	48	54
16	43	60	62	15	34	46
35	65	70	42	25	30	18
24	75	36	72	90	95	98
82	44	80	85	46	92	100

Name _____

Valentine Riddle

What did the boy elephant say to the girl elephant on Valentine's Day? To find out, solve this code. First find the answer to each addition problem. Then find the letter that matches the number in the answer. The first one is done for you.

1	2	3	4	5	6	7	8	9	10
E	I	V	N	Y	U	A	T	L	O

1. 1 + 1 = __2__ __I__

2. 3 + 6 = ____ ____

3. 8 + 2 = ____ ____

4. 2 + 1 = ____ ____

5. 0 + 1 = ____ ____

6. 4 + 1 = ____ ____

7. 5 + 5 = ____ ____

8. 4 + 2 = ____ ____

9. 1 + 6 = ____ ____

10. 3 + 5 = ____ ____

11. 7 + 3 = ____ ____

12. 2 + 2 = ____ ____

Write the letters again in order from 1 to 12.

___ ___ ___ ___ ___ ___ ___ ___ ___ ___ ___ ___!

Name _____

Problem solving with subtraction
Middle Math

Here are math stories for you to complete. The beginning and
ending of the story are here. You need to write a middle part.
You will need to use addition or subtraction to figure out what to write.

Example: Bob had 10 valentines.
             <u>Six friends gave him valentines at the party.</u>
             At the end of the party, Bob had 16 cards.

1. Mary took 14 cupcakes to the party.

   _____

   Altogether, the class had 25 cupcakes for their party.

2. Jim made 7 cards to take to the nursing home.

   _____

   So Jim and Alex took 15 cards in all.

3. Mom gave Jawan 50¢ to buy milk at school.

   _____

   Jawan gave his mother 15¢ in change.

4. Anita bought 14 valentine stickers.

   _____

   Then she had 19 stickers in all.

5. Mrs. Sharp asked 6 students to hang balloons for the party.

   _____

   Altogether, she asked 15 students to help.

6. The mailman brought 5 valentines on Monday.

   _____

   So altogether, Maria had 11 valentines.

Presidents' Day

The third Monday each February is celebrated as Presidents' Day. It is a time to especially honor GeorgeWashington, who was born on February 22, 1732; and Abraham Lincoln, who was born on February 12, 1809.

Make your own classroom murals with the background information that follows. Write each sentence on a large sheet of blank paper. Ask a pair of students to make a drawing or painting for each point. Then hang the drawings in order along a wall in your classroom or hallway.

George Washington
1. George Washington was born on February 22, 1732, on his family's large plantation (farm) in Virginia.
2. As George grew up, he learned about farming from his father.
3. George learned to find better ways to raise crops and animals.
4. George learned to make wise decisions, and these skills helped him to be a good military leader.
5. Washington became the commander-in-chief of the American army during the American Revolution.
6. Then George Washington became the first President of the United States.
7. He is often called "The Father of His Country."

Abraham Lincoln
1. Abraham Lincoln was born on February 12, 1809, in a log cabin in Kentucky.
2. Abe's father was a carpenter and a farmer.
3. When Abe was 7, his family moved to Indiana, and later they moved to Illinois.
4. Abe loved to read and would rather read a book than work in the fields.
1. Lincoln held different jobs, such as running a store, working as a postmaster and surveying land.
6. In 1834, Abraham Lincoln was elected to help make Illinois laws. Later he was elected to the national Congress.
7. In 1861, Abraham Lincoln became the 16th President of the United States.

Name Tags

Cut-Out Name Badges: Allow students to select one to wear on Presdents' Day.

I'm Celebrating Presidents' Day!

_____
name

I Love Our President!

_____
name

I'm Wishing You... a Happy Presidents' Day!

_____
Student's name

I'm Voting for

_____
as my favorite President!

Signed:

Name _____

Lincoln's Letters

Did you notice that Abe Lincoln's last name has two Ls in it? At the beginning,
you can hear the L sound. But the second L is silent. Other words have silent letters, too.
Look at the pictures. Say the words.
If you can hear the letter at the top of the box, circle it. If it is silent, cross it out.

L sidewalk	K skate	G gnat
W wrist	B table	N knee
L half	G night	L wolf
B thumb	L talk	G wagon

Name _____

Map skills, reading comprehension
Lost and Found

Thad and his family are going to see a Presidents' Day program. Thad went to get a drink, and now he is lost. Circle the right answers to help him find his family.

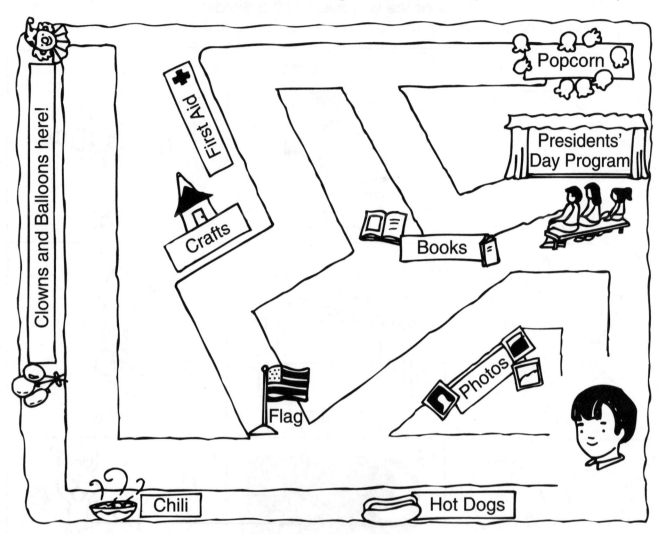

1. Where should Thad walk first?

   to the hot dogs   to the flag   ·   to the chili

2. Next, Thad should walk to the _____.

   photos   clowns   crafts

3. Thad then needs to walk to the _____.

   first aid   chili   books

4. Thad will see his family on the bench if he walks by the _____.

   popcorn   books   clowns

TLC10408 Copyright © Teaching & Learning Company, Carthage, IL 62321-0010

Name _____

Abraham Lincoln

Read the sentences below to learn more about Abraham Lincoln and Presidents' Day. Use a *past tense* verb if the sentence already happened. Use a *present tense* verb if it is happening now.

1. Abraham Lincoln (was, is) born on February 12, 1809.

2. He (grows, grew) up in a log cabin in Kentucky.

3. He (worked, works) on a farm.

4. As he grew older, Abe knew he (loves, loved) to read books more than he (loves, loved) to work in the fields.

5. Abe (holds, held) different jobs, such as postmaster and store owner.

6. Later, in 1861, Lincoln (became, becomes) President of the United States.

7. Now, we (enjoyed, enjoy) learning about his life.

8. His memory (lives, lived) on in books and movies.

9. My friend, Sam, (loves, loved) to read books about Lincoln.

10. Today, we (are, were) all glad Lincoln was our President.

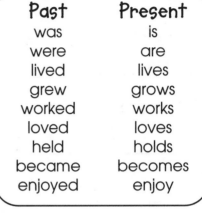

Past	Present
was	is
were	are
lived	lives
grew	grows
worked	works
loved	loves
held	holds
became	becomes
enjoyed	enjoy

Name _____

Research, writing a report

My Favorite President

Learn about some of our past United States Presidents. Which one is your favorite?

A. Look in books to find out the following information:

1. Name _____

2. Date of birth _____   Date of death _____

3. Place of birth _____

4. Facts about his family and childhood _____

_____

_____

_____

5. Jobs he had before becoming President _____

_____

6. Year he took office _____   Year he left office _____

7. Most important things he did while President _____

_____

_____

B. Now use some of the information you found to write a report. Use three paragraphs for your report:

First paragraph: Give the name of your President, his date and place of birth and some information about his family and childhood.

Second paragraph: Tell about his jobs before becoming President, and when and/or how he became President.

Third paragraph: Write about the most important things he did while President, and why he is your favorite President.

Note: You will probably not use all of the information you found in writing your report.

Name _____

President Cents
Coins show the heads of past Presidents.
Look at the chart to find out what President is on each coin.

These friends are playing a game for Presidents' Day. Each one has a certain amount of money in his or her hand. Can you tell by the clues how much money is in each person's hand? Remember to use the ¢ or $ in each answer. The first one is done for you.

1¢	5¢	10¢	25¢	50¢
penny	nickel	dime	quarter	half dollar
Lincoln	Jefferson	Roosevelt	Washington	Kennedy

1. Clare says, "I have 2 Lincolns and 1 Washington." Clare has 27¢.

2. Tony says, "I have 3 Roosevelts and 1 Lincoln." Tony has _____.

3. "I am holding 1 Kennedy and 2 Jeffersons," says Ramona. She has _____.

4. "In my hand are 2 Washingtons, 2 Roosevelts and 1 Lincoln," says Kate. She has _____.

5. Marco says, "I have 1 Washington, 3 Roosevelts and 1 Jefferson." He has _____.

6. Amber tells her friends, "I have 4 Kennedys and 4 Lincolns." She has _____.

7. "I am holding 4 Washingtons, 4 Roosevelts and 10 Lincolns," says Jamal. He has _____.

8. Lucy states, "I have 2 Kennedys, 2 Washingtons and 12 Lincolns." She has _____.

9. Ralph says, "I have 4 Kennedys, 2 Washingtons and 5 Roosevelts." He has _____.

10. Natasha says, "I have a really hard puzzle for you. Can you solve it? I had 5 Washingtons, but I spent two of them. I had 3 Roosevelts, but I gave 2 of them away. I still have 2 Jeffersons and 3 Lincolns along with the rest of the Washingtons and Roosevelts. Do you know how much money I have now?"

Can you figure this out? How much money does Natasha have? _____

Finding fractional parts of words
Hidden President

Almost everyone knows that George Washington was the first President of the United States. Do you know who was the second President? To find out, follow the instructions to use certain parts of the words below.

First name:

1. Use the first 1/4 of JUMP. ____

2. Use the last 1/2 of GO. ____

3. Use the first 1/3 of HAT. ___

4. Use the last 1/4 of BARN. ____

Last name:

5. Use the first 1/5 of APPLE. ____

6. Use the last 1/4 of GLAD. ____

7. Use the last 1/3 of BOA. ____

8. Use the first 1/4 of MAKE. ____

9. Use the first 1/5 of SNAKE. ____

The second President was __ __ __ __ __   __ __ __ __ __ __.

Pancake Day

Pancake Day is observed the day before Ash Wednesday, which marks the beginning of Lent. Pancake Day may fall in either February or March. The day is also known as Shrove Tuesday. Celebrate the continuing popularity of this food anytime during late February or early March.

Of course, your students will want to make pancakes on Pancake Day! Here are a few recipes to help you get started.

Note: Always check your students' records for food allergies. Always be sure that an adult handles the griddle, stove or other hot items.

Basic Pancake Recipe

Ingredients:
2 cups flour
3 teaspoons baking powder
$1/2$ teaspoon salt (do not omit)
$1/4$ cup sugar
2 eggs
2 tablespoons oil
1 cup milk

Instructions:
Combine dry ingredients in a bowl. (Sift if you like.) Combine liquid ingredients in a different bowl. (Ask students to decide which ingredients are dry and which are liquid.) Add the liquid ingredients all at once to the dry. Stir with a wire whisk or spoon until mixed. Do not beat. Rub griddle or frying pan with a small amount of oil. Heat until water dropped from your hand bounces around. Drop one large mixing spoonful of batter for each pancake. Cook until bubbled all over the top and brown on the bottom. Flip, cook until brown on other side. Keep the griddle at a high temperature at all times.

Variations:
1. Add $3/4$ cup blueberries or $1/2$ cup walnut pieces with dry ingredients.
2. Substitute 1 cup whole wheat flour for white flour.
3. Substitute buttermilk for whole milk and 1 teaspoon baking soda for $1/2$ teaspoon baking powder.

Also consider using a purchased baking mix such as Bisquick™. Many muffin mixes, such as Jiffy® Corn Muffin Mix have recipes for pancake batter on the package.

Gluten-Free Pancakes

Use this recipe if you have students who cannot eat wheat flour.

Gluten-Free Pancakes

Ingredients:
1 cup rice or millet flour
$1/2$ cup soy flour
$1/2$ cup cornmeal
1 tablespoon non-alum baking powder
1 egg, beaten
$1 1/2$ cups water
2 tablespoons unrefined vegetable oil

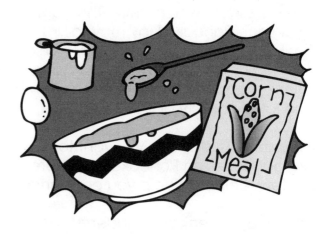

Instructions:
Combine all dry ingredients. Stir together all liquids. (Again, ask students to tell if ingredients are "dry" or "liquid.") Combine both mixtures. Stir only until dry ingredients are moistened. Drop by large spoonfuls onto griddle, preheated to 350°-375°F. Cook until bubbled all over the top and brown on the bottom. Flip, cook until brown on other side.

Pancake Topping Ideas

honey
butter or margarine
maple syrup
warmed applesauce
strawberry syrup
blueberry syrup
wheat germ

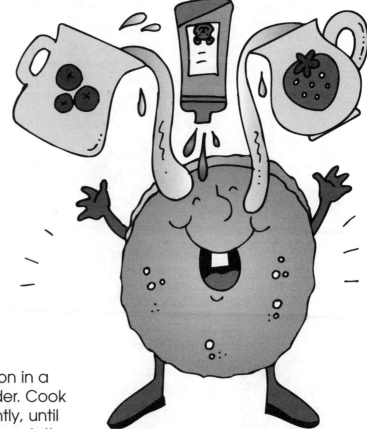

Cider Syrup

Ingredients:
1 cup sugar
2 tablespoons cornstarch
$1/2$ teaspoon ground cinnamon
2 cups apple cider
2 tablespoons margarine or butter

Instructions:
Mix sugar, cornstarch and cinnamon in a one-quart saucepan. Stir in the cider. Cook over medium heat, stirring constantly, until the mixture thickens and boils. Boil and stir for 1 minute. Remove from the heat; stir in the margarine. Delicious on top of pancakes, waffles or ice cream!

Shape Book Pattern

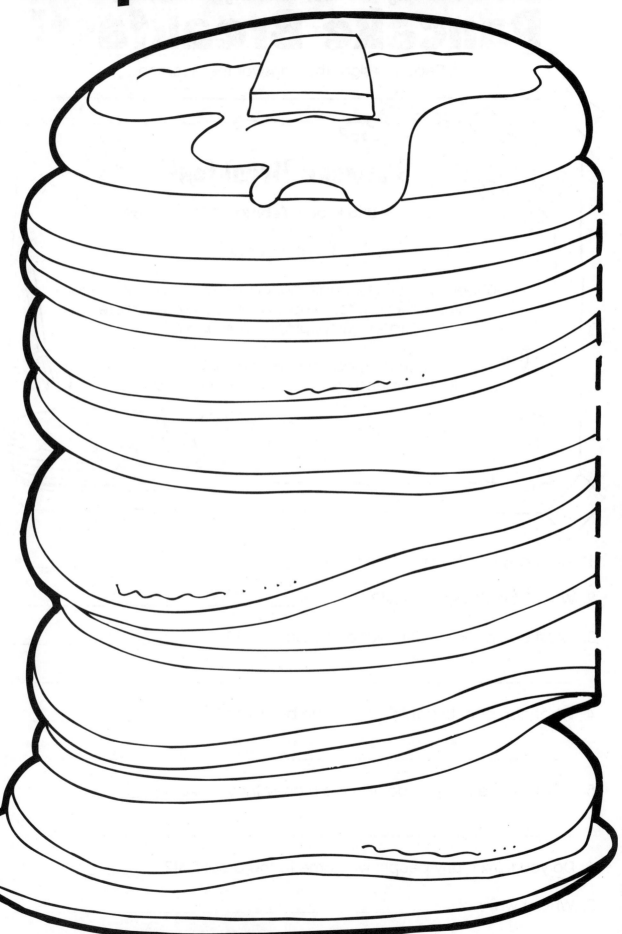

Name _____

Pancake Breakfast!

Read the sign. Then answer the questions.

Pancake Breakfast

Thursday and Friday, February 27th and 28th
7 a.m. to 9 a.m.
$3.00 per person

Blueberry pancakes, apple pancakes, sausage and bacon
Maple syrup, cider syrup, honey, butter and more
Orange juice, grape juice and milk

Pancakes made by Elm School 2nd graders
Money raised will go for City Homeless Shelter

1. What days will the pancake breakfast be held? _____

2. What time is the breakfast? _____

3. What can people get to eat at the breakfast? _____

   _____

4. What can people get to drink at the breakfast? _____

   _____

5. What will the students do with the money they make? _____

   _____

6. Do you think many people will come to the breakfast? _____

7. Why or why not? _____

Name _____

Drawing conclusions, making judgments
Pancake Party

Sometimes you have enough facts to draw a conclusion. Sometimes you don't.
Read each example below. Circle the correct answer.

1. Everyone in the class is helping to make pancakes. Julie is in my class. Is Julie helping to make pancakes?

   Yes   No   You can't tell

2. Mrs. Jones wants to stay and help make pancakes. She has to be at work at 10:00. We will start making pancakes at 10:30. Will Mrs. Jones be staying to help us?

   Yes   No   You can't tell

3. Jimmy only likes Red Delicious apples. We are making apple pancakes. Will Jimmy like our pancakes?

   Yes   No   You can't tell

4. People who have washed their hands can help make pancakes. Sara did not wash her hands. Can she help make pancakes?

   Yes   No   You can't tell

5. We started with a 10-pound bag of flour. We made 2 batches of pancakes. Do we have 5 pounds of flour leftover?

   Yes   No   You can't tell

6. Everyone who helped make pancakes were allowed to eat them. Ray helped make pancakes. Was Ray allowed to eat them?

   Yes   No   You can't tell

Name _____

Find the Most

Look at each picture. Circle the object that holds the most.

Name _____

Multiplication
How Many Pancakes?

Mr. Chef's third grade class is making a pancake breakfast for their parents. Read each problem and answer the question about the supplies they will need.

1. One recipe for apple pancakes calls for 2 apples. If the students make 4 batches of that recipe, how many apples will they need?

2. Another recipe for cornmeal pancakes calls for 3 tablespoons of oil. If Mr. Chef's class makes 4 batches of cornmeal pancakes, how much oil will they use?

3. The banana recipe calls for $1/2$ cup of sugar. How much sugar will the second graders need if they make two batches of banana pancakes?

4. The class wants to make 3 batches of oatmeal raisin pancakes, and each batch calls for 2 cups of raisins. Harry can bring 1 cup of raisins. Sally can also bring 1 cup of raisins. How many more cups of raisins do the students need?

5. Mr. Chef can buy paper plates in packages of 10. If he buys 5 packages, how many paper plates will they have?

6. The class can buy paper cups in packages of 8. If they buy 6 packages, how many cups will they have?

7. Maria can pour 6 glasses of orange juice from each pitcher. How many glasses can she pour from 5 pitchers?

8. Colin's mother can make 9 pancakes at a time on one griddle. How many pancakes can she make on 3 griddles?

All-Purpose February

Use this bulletin board idea for the entire month of February. See pages 123-124 for patterns.

Place a large heart (for Valentine's Day) behind the title of the display. Add a presidential silhouette for Presidents' Day and another silhouette for Groundhog Day. Patterns for these can be found on pages 123-124. Also include a large light bulb for Edison's birthday and a scroll for Black History Month.

Black History Month

Edison's Birthday Feb. 11

Groundhog Day

February 2

Presidents' Day

February _____

Bookmarks & Awards

Use these bookmarks and awards during the special days in February.

Early Spring or More Winter? Spend It Reading!

I Light Up with a good book!

February 11th is Edison's Birthday

Dear _____,

I **L O V e** your work!

Congratulations on your good efforts!

From,

_____

This award is for

_____

for

Outstanding work during **Black History Month**

Date:

Signed:

March

Get ready for a marvelous March! Here is a fresh assortment of bulletin boards, teacher helps and curriculum reproducible pages to see you through many of the special days in March.

We've chosen six special themes: Umbrella Month, National Pig Day, Save Your Vision Week, Saint Patrick's Day, the first day of spring and National Bubble Week. For some of these themes you will find bulletin boards, songs, action poems and resource lists. For all of the units you will have appealing reproducibles that cover important primary level skills. Most skill sheets are for math or language, but we've also included some pages for science, social studies and general thinking skills.

Pick the themes you are most interested in and select activities and worksheets that are on an appropriate level for your students. You will be able to use many ideas in each unit even though some individual pages may be too difficult or too simple for your particular class. You can copy the reproducible pages directly from the book. The bulletin board patterns, stationery and other items are included on the CD and numbered for easy reference.

First your students will learn "umbrella etiquette" and weather words. They can help you complete a bulletin board, keep a weather calendar and practice reading and math skills, too.

Pigs are the feature of the second section. These farm animals are not just about mud and slime—they're for learning, too! Choose several picture books from the resource list to read to your students on National Pig Day. Teach your students about pigs and pork and cows and beef using suggestions found on the teacher page. You can also cover science, language and math skills as well.

The "Save Your Vision Week" portion includes tips for classroom games and some fun reproducibles on analogies, Venn diagrams and more. The teacher page lists some important tips you can share with your students on good eye care.

No book about March would be complete without tipping our hats to the Irish and St. Patrick's Day. A bulletin board idea is included here, some fun pages about a leprechaun's hat and an Irish map page. You'll also find a tricky letter code and a page of word problems. Art ideas and party suggestions are included on the teacher page.

The first day of spring is featured in the fifth section, beginning with an action poem and a fingerplay. Story writing, a word search puzzle and baby animal names are some of the activities for this time of new beginnings.

National Bubble Week completes the special observances for March. This is a high-interest topic which lends itself easily to many science activities. Included are just a few ideas and worksheets. With these ideas as launching points, you're bound to "bubble over" with many more educational ideas of your own!

Don't forget all the great bonus clip art on the CD. It promises to make for a truly marvelous March in your classroom!

Umbrella Month

Don't get wet, get an umbrella! Have fun with this wonderful invention as you work with your students on important springtime skills. If possible, bring several different umbrellas into your classroom to use in these activities:

1. Teach "umbrella etiquette," including these tips:

   - Do not open an umbrella until you are completely outside.

   - When you come inside, close your wet umbrella right away and leave it near the door.

   - Do not put a wet umbrella on a bus seat or any place where someone may want to sit.

   - When two people are sharing an umbrella, the taller person should carry it.

   - When walking with an umbrella, hold it up, not out.

   - Be very careful not to bump people with your umbrella when walking in busy places.

2. Have students act out proper umbrella manners. Put students in groups of two or three and ask each group to demonstrate one of the points above.

3. Show your students two different umbrellas. Ask questions such as:
   How are these two umbrellas alike?
   How are they different?
   Would one of them work better than the other? Why or why not?
   Which one would you rather use? Why?
   How many people can fit under each umbrella?

4. Make these "edible umbrellas" for a special March treat:
   Purchase several small tubes of colored icing from the bakery section of your grocery store. Also purchase a box of plain graham crackers or other large flat crackers or cookies. Let each student decorate his cracker by squeezing out an umbrella shape with one color and then adding other colors for stripes or polka dots. If blue icing is available, some students may even want to add raindrops.

Note: Very young students may have difficulty making a good outline with the tube of icing, so the teacher or other helpers may need to do the basic outline on the cracker. Then let the children simply add the extra decorations.

Umbrella Month

Use the patterns on page 129 for this bulletin board. Cut a large cloud from white paper and write "Wether Words" on it or use the pattern on the CD. Tack it to the middle of the board. Tell each student to cut out an umbrella and a raindrop. He should write one weather word on the front of each and his name on the back. Add all the umbrellas and raindrops to the display. See how many different words your students can name. You may wish to allow students to add more shapes and weather words throughout the month of March.

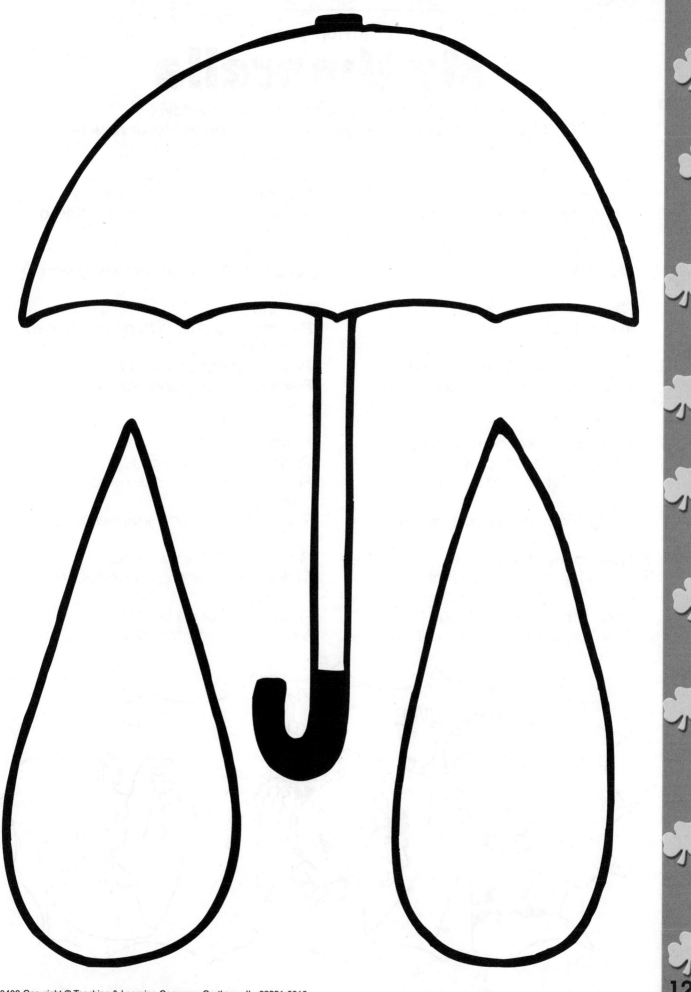

Name _____

My Umbrella

Use this poem inside on a really rainy day.
Or, if the weather permits, try practicing it outside with your students.

I put up my umbrella
When the raindrops start to fall.

(Pretend to put up umbrella.)
(Make falling raindrops with fluttering
    fingertips.)

I try to keep myself all dry,
My head, my coat and all.

(Point to self.)
(Point to head, coat and whole body.)

I like to splish and splash
In puddles large and small

(March.)
(Put arms together in large circle, then
    small circle.)

So I must wear big boots you see,
That are both strong and tall.

(Pretend to put on boots.)
(Flex muscle for strong. Reach high for
    tall.)

My umbrella keeps my hair all dry,
My arms and legs as well
But my feet are not so simple

(Lightly tap hair.)
(Point to arms and legs.)
(Point to feet and shake head back and
    forth.)

So my mom thinks boots are swell!

(Raise eyebrows and smile widely.)

I put up my umbrella
When the rain begins to fall.

(Pretend to put up umbrella.)
(Make falling raindrops with fluttering
    fingertips.)

And I put on my big, tough boots
Then splash and have a ball!

(Pretend to put on boots.)
(March with feet and clap hands.)

Name _____

Raindrops

Max and Molly like to watch the raindrops. Can you help them find the
biggest and smallest raindrops? Circle the five biggest raindrops.
Put an X on the five smallest raindrops. Then color the entire picture.

Short u and long u sounds
The Unicorn's Umbrella

This silly unicorn is holding an umbrella! What do you think of that? Both *unicorn* and *umbrella* begin with the letter *u*, but both have a very different sound.
The sound that *u* makes in *unicorn* is called the long *u* sound.
The sound that it makes in *umbrella* is called the short *u* sound.
Say the name of each picture below.
If the *u* makes the long *u* sound, circle the unicorn.
If the *u* makes the short *u* sound, circle the umbrella.

cup	sun	uniform
music	gum	human
United States	bus	rug

Name _____

Words with double letters
Double Trouble

Umbrella is a word with double letters.
Here are some more double-letter words that you may know:

penny   dress   mitten   juggle

Add a set of double letters to spell these
words. Look at the picture box for clues
to help you.

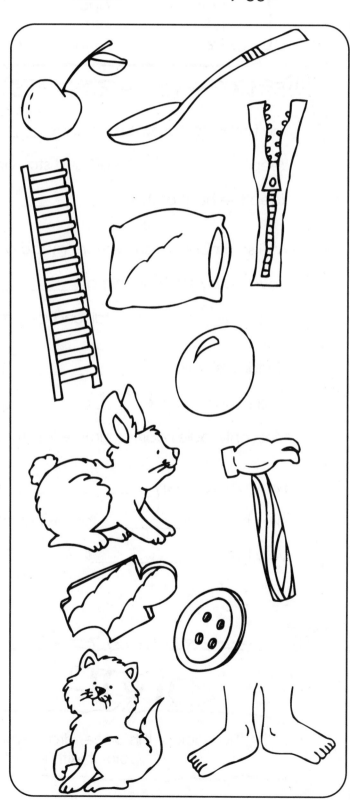

1. r a _ _ i t

2. p u _ _ l e

3. k i _ _ e n

4. h a _ _ e r

5. p i _ _ o w

6. s p _ _ n

7. b u _ _ o n

8. c h e _ _ y

9. l a _ _ e r

10. z i _ _ e r

11. f _ _ t

12. e _ _

Name _____

The Umbrella

Read this article about the umbrella. Find a word in the word box below that makes sense for each blank in the story. Write the correct word in each space.

wood	ago	family	made
rain	other	umbrellas	sun
first	thankful	day	skin

The umbrella has two main uses. _____, many people use it to

keep _____ off and stay dry. Secondly, some people use it to

keep the heat of the _____ off.

At first, umbrella frames were made of _____, and they were

covered by cloth or animal _____. Now, frames are usually

_____ of metal, and they may be covered with cloth or plastic.

Hundreds of years _____, in some countries, only the priests

and ministers carried _____. Later in _____ coun-

tries, only ladies carried umbrellas. These umbrellas were called *parasols*.

Now almost every _____ has one or more umbrellas, and we

are all _____ for this invention, especially on a very rainy or

very hot _____!

On the back of this page, draw an interesting design for an umbrella.
Color it with lots of different colors.

Weather and calendar skills

March Weather

Complete this calendar for the month of March. First write the names of the days of the week at the top. Then add the numbers for the dates in the correct boxes. During the month, add a picture to each day of your calendar to show what the weather was like.

	= sunny		= cloudy		= thunderstorm
	= partly cloudy		= rain		= snow

Name _____

Counting and adding
Polka-Dot Umbrellas

Look at all these polka-dot umbrellas! Count how many dots are on each umbrella.
Add more dots to equal the number written under each umbrella.

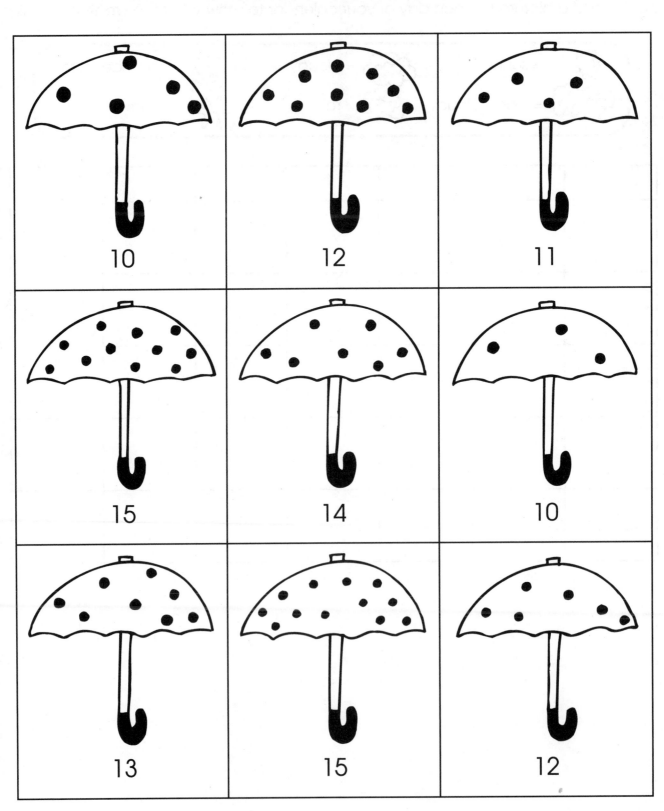

Name _____

Less than, greater than
More or Less

In each box below, the first group of rain items has less than the second group, or more than the second group. Write the correct sign in the blanks.

< less than   > more than

👢 boots (4) ____ boots (3)	💧 raindrops (7) ____ raindrops (8)
🧥 coats (5) ____ coats (6)	☂ umbrellas (8) ____ umbrellas (8)
💧 raindrops (8) ____ raindrops (8)	👢 boots (7) ____ boots (8)
☂ umbrellas (8) ____ umbrellas (6)	🟠 clouds (4) ____ clouds (4)

Name _____

Subtracting with regrouping

Subtract and Color

Here is a hidden picture puzzle for you to solve. First, find the answer to each subtraction problem and write it in each space with your pencil. Then use a crayon to color all the spaces with answers that are less than 10. How many umbrellas will you color?

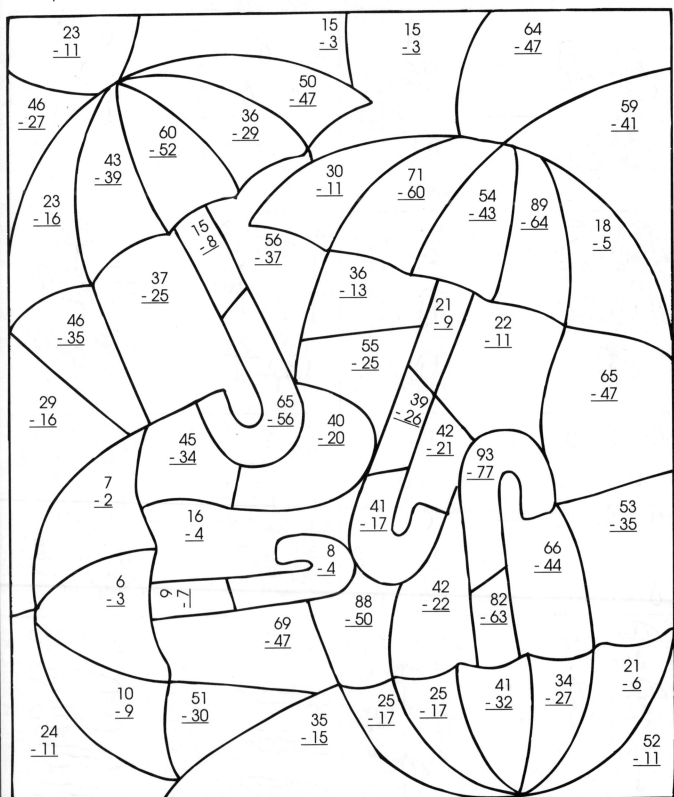

138

TLC10408 Copyright © Teaching & Learning Company, Carthage, IL 62321-0010

National Pig Day

Here's a day to celebrate a very important animal, the pig! We often think of pigs as being filthy, but pigs actually wallow in mud to seek relief from the heat due to their ineffective sweat glands. Pigs that are given a clean environment that is sheltered from the sun remain very clean. And while pigs suffer from a reputation for being stupid, in reality these animals are very intelligent. Some studies report that they are more intelligent than dogs. Pigs are economically important because they are the source of a wide variety of meats, leather, sturdy bristles for many kinds of brushes and many medical products.

Here are some ideas to help you celebrate National Pig Day with your students:

• Invite a pork producer to visit your classroom and talk about how they raise healthy hogs. Ask them to talk about what pigs eat, how long it takes them to mature, etc.

• If possible, visit a farm where pigs are raised.

• Talk about foods that come from pigs. Explain the pork comes from pigs. List products such as pork sausage and hot dogs, ham, pork chops, bacon, etc. Then explain that beef comes from cows and list beef products. Cook some pork products to eat in class. Ask volunteers to come in and help students make bacon, lettuce and tomato sandwiches or sausage and pancakes.

• Teach these terms to your students:
hogs, swine—other terms for pigs
boar—male pigs
sow—female pigs
litter—a group of young animals born at the same time
omnivores—animals that eat both plant and animal products. Pigs are omnivores. Wild pigs eat a wide variety of foods, including leaves, roots, fruit and rodents. Domestic pigs eat such foods as corn, grain, potatoes, dairy by-products, commercial feeds and edible garbage.

• Sing "Old MacDonald Had a Farm."

• Read "The Three Little Pigs." See page 144 for more activities related to this fable.

• Read E.B. White's classic children's story, *Charlotte's Web*. It is always a favorite with primary students.

Shape Book Pattern

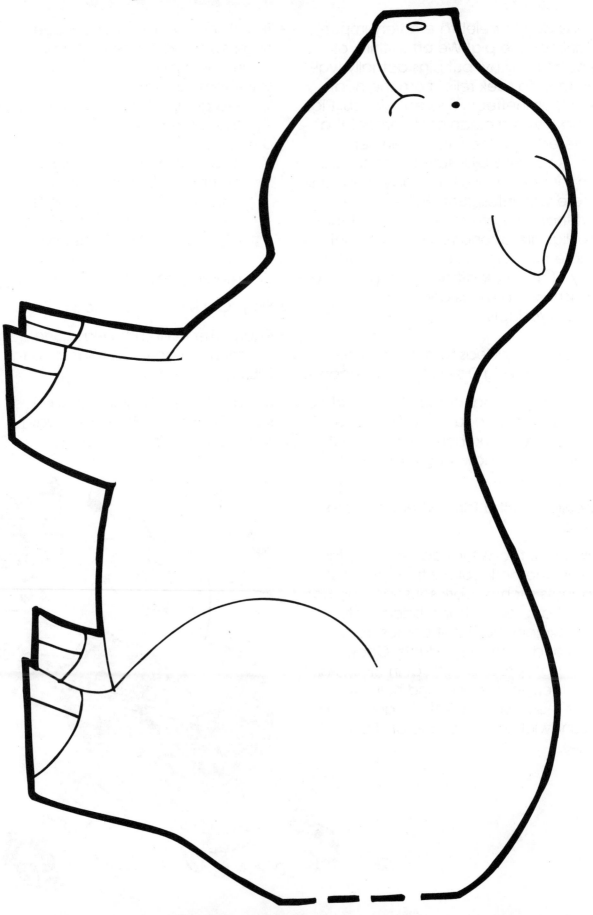

Name _____

Pigpen

Pigs often live in areas called pens. Do you hear the *p* sound at the beginning of *pig* and *pen*? Lots of other three-letter words begin with *P* as well. Here are some examples:

pat   pit   pad   pod   pea   pet

Can you think of any more? _____

Now look at each set of letters. Circle the letter that can
be used to make three real words. The first one is done for you.

1.	2.	3.
f c (p) __ig __en __at	h r t __un __ag __ed	l b c __eg __id __ot
4.	5.	6.
f j k __am __ug __ar	m s w __ap __ud __ob	d g s __un __at __ip
7.	8.	9.
h l m __ot __is __am	r t y __et __es __am	f n z __ot __ap __et
10.	11.	12.
b s w __ig __ag __as	c h t __en __ar __ip	b p m __ig __ag __ug

Name _____

Farm Time

Here are some pictures and words that you might see on a pig farm.
Look very carefully at the words. Circle the one in each row that is spelled correctly.
Then write it on the line. The first one is done for you.

barn	banr	darn	burn	barn
gaot	goat	got	gate	_____
chuck	check	chick	chik	_____
hay	ha	haye	hiy	_____
carn	korn	cirn	corn	_____
duck	dack	duk	buck	_____
farmr	firmer	farmer	fermr	_____
gras	grass	grasss	griss	_____
horse	harse	hores	hors	_____

Now make your own farm picture on the back of this page.
Write a sentence using one or more of the words you wrote above.

Name _____

Where's the Pig?

Where are the animals on this farm? Finish each sentence with a word from the word box.

1. The pig is _____ his

2. The cow is resting in the shade, _____ the

Word Box
across
under
in
around
to
on

3. An owl sits _____ the

4. The chicken runs _____ the

5. A goat is tied _____ the

6. A horse gallops _____ the

143

Name _____

Understanding story order/making a story map

The Three Little Pigs

Listen while your teacher reads to you a version of the story, "The Three Little Pigs."
Then complete this story map for the story you just heard.

Story Title	_____
Characters	_____ _____ _____
Important Events	_____ _____ _____ _____ _____ _____ _____ _____ _____ _____ _____ _____ _____ _____
Ending	_____ _____ _____

Name _____

Comparing weights
Weigh to Measure!

Look at the animals in the first box. Which one do you think is the heaviest?
Circle it. Then circle the heaviest object in each of the other boxes.

Multiplication
Pig Count

Help Farmer Brown count his pigs. For each picture of a pigpen, write a multiplication problem. Then find the answer and write it in the blank. The first one is done for you.

$$4 \times 2 = 8$$

_____

_____

_____

_____

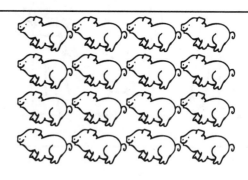

_____

_____

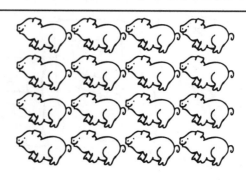

_____

TLC10408 Copyright © Teaching & Learning Company, Carthage, IL 62321-0010

Name _____

Science: Animal foods
Hungry Animals

Animals eat many different foods. Pigs on farms eat mostly corn and grains, but in the wild they also eat reptiles and rodents. Look at the pictures here. Fill in the name of one of those animals in each sentence below. Color the pictures.

Use one of these words in the blanks. Use each word only once:
lion   bird   sheep   rabbit

1. A _____ and a _____ eat plants.

2. A _____ eats animals.

3. A sometimes _____ eats both animals and plants.

4. Can you think of another animal that eats plants? _____

5. Can you name another animal that eats animals? _____

Draw pictures of these animals on the back of this page.

Resources

Retellings of "The Three Little Pigs"

For a "fractured" version with a different ending, try *The Three Pigs* by David Wiesner. Houghton Mifflin Company, 2001.

For a tale told from the wolf's point of view, read *The True Story of the 3 Little Pigs* by Jon Scieszka, et al. Penguin Putnam Books for Young Readers, 1996.

Here's a book that incorporates math and geometry skills and even a tangram puzzle: *Three Pigs, One Wolf, and Seven Magic Shapes: Level 3* by Grace Maccarone, et al. Scholastic, Inc., 1997.

This book is a hilarious turn-about tale where the wolves are small and helpless and the pig is big and bad: *The Three Little Wolves and the Big Bad Pig* by Eugene Trivizas. Simon & Schuster Children's, 1997.

Read one of these for a more classic version of the beloved fable: *The Three Little* by Betty Miles. Simon & Schuster Children's, 1998.

The Three Little Pigs by James Marshall. Penguin Putnam Books for Young Readers, 2000.

Other Fun Pig Stories

If You Give a Pig a Pancake by Laura Joffe Numeroff. HarperCollins Publishers, 1998.

The Little Pig by Judy Dunn. Random House Books for Young Readers, 1987.

Pigs Aplenty, Pigs Galore! by David M. McPhail. Penguin Putnam Books for Young Readers, 1996.

Informational Books

Pigs by Gail Gibbons. Holiday House, Inc., 2000.

Pigs in the Pantry: Fun with Math and Cooking by Amy Axelrod. Aladdin Paperbacks, 1999.

The World of Farm Animals: An Early Encyclopedia for Beginning Readers by the Sterling Publishing Company, Sterling Publishing Co., Inc., 2002.

Save Your Vision Week

One week in March has been proclaimed Save Your Vision Week annually since 1964. It is usually observed during the first full week of the month. This is a good time to talk with your students about important things they can do to keep their eyes healthy. Here are some tips to pass along:

• Have an eye exam once a year.

• Never put anything sharp in your eye. Do not run with scissors or other sharp objects that might accidentally hurt another person's eyes.

• Eat a balanced diet with plenty of fresh fruits and vegetables.

• If you're out in the sun, remember to wear sunglasses and plenty of sunscreen.

• Do not look directly at the sun.

Vitamin A is one of the important nutrients for eye health. It prevents some eye diseases and night blindness. Animal fats (as found in butter, cheese and whole milk), liver and vegetables (especially green leafy vegetables and carrots) are good sources of Vitamin A. A coloring page of some of these foods is found on page 151.

You will also want to have fun with the visual puzzles on the pages that follow. Encourage your students to work on other manipulatives in your classroom such as tangrams, jigsaw puzzles and more. Here are some additional activities to do during Save Your Vision Week:

• Play "I Spy." One student selects an object within sight of the other students. He tries not to look at it but describes it in detail, according to its size, shape and color. Other students look around the room and try to guess the object. The person to guess it correctly chooses the next object.

• Draw or reproduce similar shapes on an overhead. Can your students distinguish between ones that are the same and ones that are different? Can they recognize ones that are the same shape but not the same size? Ones that are the same but in different positions, such as when one has been flipped?

• Consider hiding a special object (such as a vase, a toy car, etc.) many times during the week. Tell students that anytime they spy it, they should raise their hand and tell you. Keep track of those who succeed in finding it. Hide it again the next time you have a chance without being caught. Award a small prize (perhaps the vase or car?) at the end of the week to the person who spied the object the most times.

With very young students, you may want to review all five senses during this week. Can your students name all the senses? Do they know what body part is used for each?

Name _____

Backwards, Forwards

Which of these letters are backwards? Which are forwards? Cross out the letters that are backwards. Find all the letters that are written correctly and circle them. Choose one letter that you circled. Name three things that begin with that letter. Draw a picture of one of those objects on the back of this page.

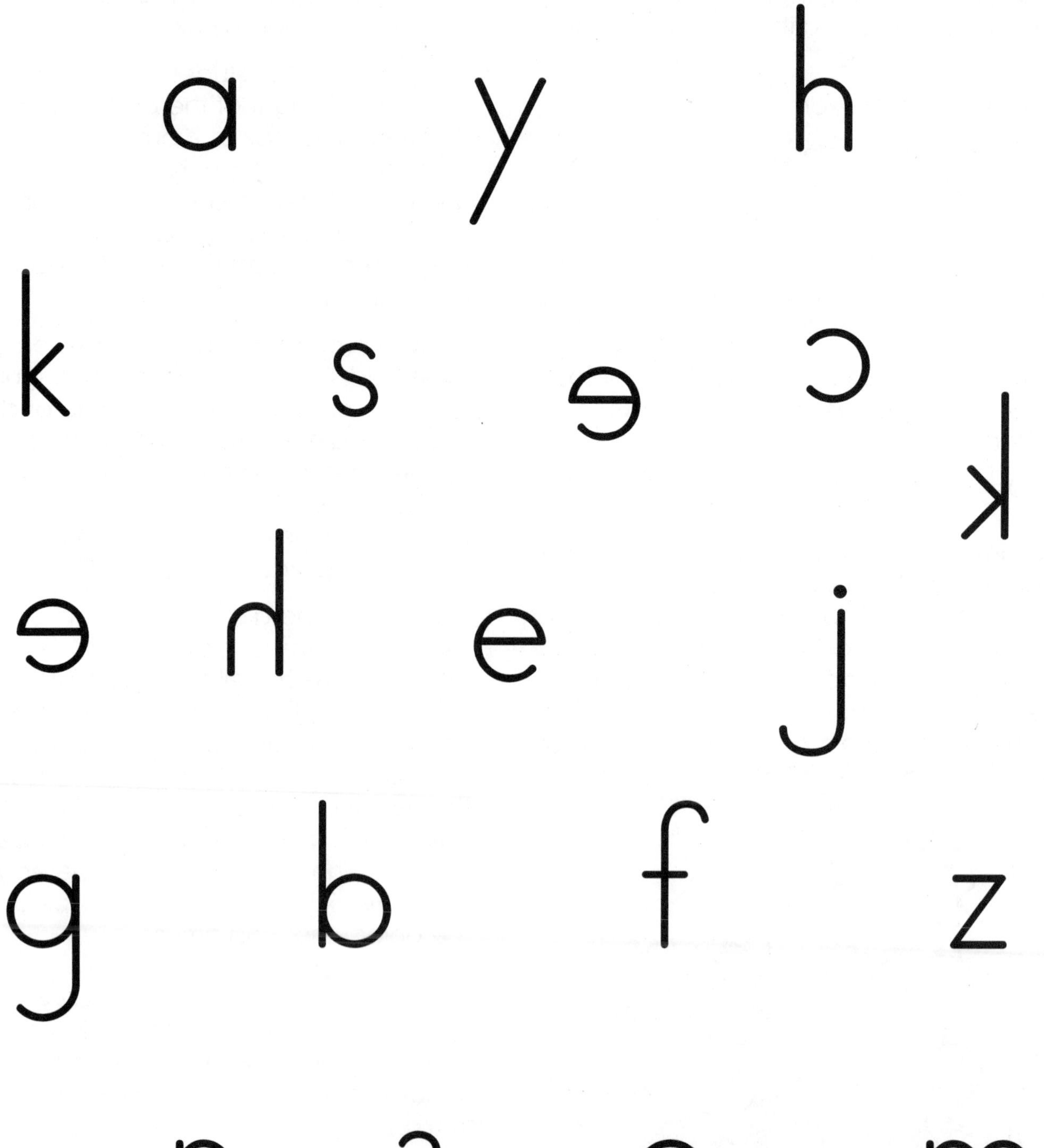

a y h

k s ɘ ɔ

ǝ ᖯ e ʞ j

g b f z

r ƨ c m

TLC10408 Copyright © Teaching & Learning Company, Carthage, IL 62321-0010

Name _____

Nutrition
Healthy Eyes

Your eyes need some special healthy foods to help them work properly. Foods that have some animal fat and many vegetables, especially carrots and green leafy ones, are very good for your eyes. In each row, color the foods that are good for your eyes.

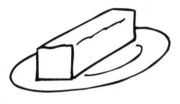  

TLC10408 Copyright © Teaching & Learning Company, Carthage, IL 62321-0010

Analogies
What's Next?
Use your logic skills and your healthy eyes.
Decide what shape should come next in each line. Draw it in the blank space.

1.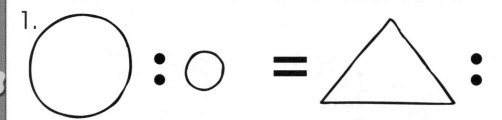

2.

3.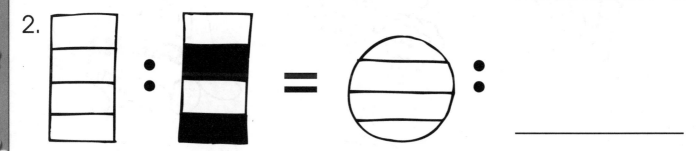

4.

5.

Name _____

Ready, Set, Go!

You will need to use your eyes very carefully to solve this puzzle!
Which picture below was made from this exact set of shapes?

Circle the number of the correct set of shapes. Then color all the circles green,
all the rectangles yellow, all the triangles blue and all the hexagons red.

Reading a Venn diagram
Eye Exam

Pretend that you are having an eye exam and the doctor shows you this chart.
Study the shapes carefully. Then answer the questions at the bottom.

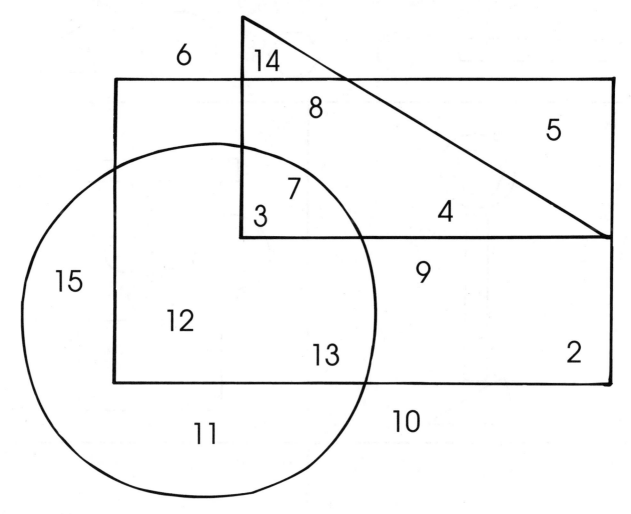

A. What numbers are in the circle, triangle and rectangle? _____

B. What numbers are in the circle but not in the triangle or rectangle?

_____

C. What numbers are in both the triangle and rectangle but not in the circle?

_____

D. What numbers are in the rectangle but not in the triangle or the circle?

_____

E. What numbers are outside all of the shapes? _____

Saint Patrick's Day

Celebrate this special Irish day with your little leprechauns. Why not try some of these ideas?

Gold Rush

If weather permits, here's a magical hunt that your young students are sure to enjoy.

Prior to St. Patrick's Day, select enough small stones or pebbles for each of your students to have one to three apiece. Clean the stones and coat them with gold spray paint. Allow stones to dry thoroughly. Then just before this event, ask a parent helper to sneak outside ahead of time to "hide" these gold stones on the playground. Then announce to your students that they are going on a special hunt. They should pretend they are leprechauns looking for magic stones. Tell them that gold stones are the best, although they are welcome to pick up other stones that they may find as well. Instruct students they are only allowed to gather 1, 2 or 3 gold stones each (according to the number of stones you prepared). Encourage them to carry them in their pockets throughout the day.

Like magic!

Green Fingerpaint

Tell students they can make their own green finger paint. Begin with these supplies:

- 1 medium resealable plastic bag
- shaving cream (white)
- blue and yellow food coloring

Squirt white shaving cream inside the plastic bag and add a few drops of food coloring. Close the bag, making sure that all the air is out. Then tell kids to mix the colors into the shaving cream with their hands. (This gives the students the opportunity to explore mixing colors, to see that blue and yellow makes green. And there's no mess to clean up afterwards!) Then snip a corner off the bag and squirt the paint out onto a piece of paper. Use as a fingerpaint for your favorite St. Patrick's Day pictures.

Magic Mushrooms

Find a blackline drawing of a large mushroom, frog, flower or other fun shape. Reproduce the drawing on bright yellow construction paper. Give students blue bingo markers, and tell them to use the markers for "magic" dots. It is magic to see the blue dots turn out green on the mushroom!

Green Lunch

Plan your classroom party food, or an entire lunch menu, around the color green. Here are some suggested foods:
kiwi fruit or apples with green skins
lettuce/salad
split pea soup
green colored milk or cottage cheese
green colored frosting on graham crackers
green finger gelatin:

Dissolve four small packages of lime gelatin in $2\frac{1}{2}$ cups of boiling water. Chill in a 9" x 13" pan. When firm, cut into squares or other "lucky" shapes.

Saint Patrick's Day

Use the patterns on page 157 for the center of the bulletin board. Explain that, "Top o' the morning," is an old Irish greeting that people might used to say, "Good morning." Ask students to think of other friendly greetings that they might use. List several on the board. Then tell each student to cut out a shamrock using the shapes on page 158. On it, he should write his choice of a friendly greeting and sign his name on the back. Alternately, you could list ways to say, "Hello," in other languages.

158

Shape Book Pattern

Logic, noting details

Lucky Hats

Lucky the Leprechaun is getting ready to celebrate St. Patrick's Day. He wants to wear just the right hat, but which one is it? Read these clues to figure out which is the hat Lucky wants to wear. When you find it, circle it. Then color all of the hats.

Clues
1. Lucky's favorite hat has a ribbon on it.
2. It has a round buckle.
3. It does not have a flower.
4. There are no stripes on Lucky's favorite hat.

Can you find the right hat?

Recognizing letters, cut-and-paste

Hooray for Ireland!

Where was Saint Patrick's Day first celebrated? It was in Ireland, of course. Look carefully at the letters below. Cut out the ones that you need to spell the word *Ireland*. When you have found all the correct letters, paste them in order onto a piece of green paper. Remember, the word you want to spell is: *Ireland*

n	g	o
n	I	d
J	r	l
e	u	T

TLC10408 Copyright © Teaching & Learning Company, Carthage, IL 62321-0010

Name _____

Irish Cities

Ireland is a beautiful, green country. While much of the island is farmland, there are also many fine cities there. Here are the names of several of Ireland's larger cities. Number them from 1 to 14 to show how they go in ABC order.

____ Dublin

____ Belfast

____ Londonderry

____ Cork

____ Limerick

____ Cavan

____ Waterford

____ Tipperary

____ Downpatrick

____ Wexford

____ Sligo

____ Killarney

____ Galway

____ Omagh

Now find the same cities on the map. Put the number that you wrote to each city on the list by the name of the city on the map.

Name _____

Adjectives
A Lucky Day

There is an old tale that says if you follow a beautiful rainbow to its end, you will find a lucky leprechaun and a big pot of gold.

The words *old, beautiful, lucky* and *big* are all adjectives. They tell more about the nouns *tale, rainbow, leprechaun* and *pot*. Adjectives describe nouns. Circle each adjective in this list. Then use one of the words you circled to finish each sentence.

long	slippery	cozy	hot
house	tree	dry	win
cold	fish	blazing	sandy
good	candy	rainbow	fun

1. Toby and his leprechaun friend were walking along a _____ beach.

   They decided to play a game by climbing on rocks.

2. The leprechaun stepped on a _____ rock.

3. Then he fell into the _____ water.

4. Toby quickly threw him a _____ rope.

5. Toby was able to pull his _____ friend out of the water.

6. Next they found a _____ towel for the leprechaun.

7. After they built a _____ fire and fixed some _____

   food to eat, the two decided to call it day.

8. Toby and the leprechaun walked back to Toby's _____ house.

9. "Next year for St. Patrick's Day," suggested the leprechaun, "let's play a

   _____ inside game!"

164

Keyboarding skills, left and right

Leprechaun Languages

Did you know that leprechauns write in their own language? Leo Leprechaun types all his messages out on a computer, but he replaces each letter that we would use with the letter that is next to it on the keyboard. For example, if you found this word in a message from Leo: *sif*, you could look at a keyboard and look for the letter that comes to the right of the letter given. Then you could spell our word: *dog*.

Try to decode these words written in Leo's language. Write our word on the blank.

1. fewwb _____

2. kyxjt _____

3. fuek _____

4. fiks _____

5. agwwo _____

6. Ueuag _____

Lola Leprechaun uses a different language. This time, you need to find the letter that comes to the left on the keyboard. (Hint: Both leprechauns used one of the same words!)

Example: jsy   hat

7. npu _____

8. dmsvl _____

9. htrrm _____

10. gim _____

Name _____

Party Preparations

Read each word problem very carefully. Then work out some math problems so that you can answer each question. Use the work space, and write your answer in the blank.

1. The third graders are having a party for March 17. Three parents each supplied a package of 10 cups. There are 27 students in the class plus 1 teacher. How many extra cups are there?

   _____

2. Sabrina's mom baked 2 dozen cookies. Will's dad baked 1 dozen cookies. If each of the 27 students plus the teacher all eat one cookie, how many extras will there be? _____

3. Each student (and the teacher, too) needs a knife and a spoon for the party. How many utensils are needed in all ? _____

4. During the party, the students will make a craft. They will need 1 small jar of paint for every 3 students. How many jars of paint are needed?

   _____

5. Fruit juice comes in cases of 8. The teacher bought 4 cases. If each one of the 27 students, plus the teacher, drink one bottle of juice, how many bottles will be leftover?

   _____

6. Tina's mom sent in 30 balloons. Jeff's grandma sent in 30 balloons, too. If every child receives 2 balloons (and the teacher does not), how many extra balloons will there be? _____

7. Bryce used 5 pieces of green construction paper to make shamrocks. He cut 3 shamrocks from each piece. The teacher put 4 of the shamrocks on the bulletin board. How many more shamrocks does Bryce have? _____

8. Betsy played Irish music on her guitar. She played 3 songs that each lasted 2 minutes. After the second song, she took a break that lasted for 1 minute. How long in all did the music take?

   _____

First Day of Spring

Use this action poem and fingerplay to start your springtime celebration.

I Like Spring
An action poem

I like robins and butterflies.
(Flap arms as if they were wings.)
I like tulips and bright, blue skies
(Look up and point to the sky.)

I like the green grass that tickles my toes
(Gently move feet around.)
And the smell of flowers
that reach my nose.
(Inhale deeply.)

I like blossoms and flowery scenes.
(Pretend to look through binoculars.)
I like Easter and jelly beans.
(Pat tummy.)

I like bunnies and chocolate eggs
*(Place hands at top of
head like rabbit ears.)*
I like to run and stretch my legs.
(Run in place.)

I like warmth and everything.
(Hug yourself and rub your arms.)
I like you and I like spring!
(Point to another student and then clap.)

Ten Little Bunnies
A fingerplay

(Hold up the number of fingers mentioned in the rhyme.)

One little bunny sitting in the dew
Another bunny joins him and then there
   are two.
Two little bunnies as happy as can be,
Another comes along and then there are
   three.
Three little bunnies looking for more,
One joins the fun and then there are four.
Four little bunnies sniffing a beehive.
Another joins them and then there are
   five.
Five little bunnies playing some tricks,
One joins the fun and then there are six.
Six little bunnies that belong to Devin.
He finds another, and then there are
   seven.
Seven little bunnies who just can't wait
For their cousin to join them, and then
   there are eight.
Eight little bunnies hopping in a line.
Another one hops in and then there are
   nine.
Nine little bunnies hopping once again.
One more comes and then there are ten.
Ten little bunnies who really like to play
Till a loud dog barks and scares them all
   away!

Name _____

Kite Flight

Four friends are having fun flying their kites on a breezy spring day. First color
each child's shirt to match the color word under the picture. Then trace the kite strings
to find out who is flying which kite. Color the kites the same color as its owner's shirt.

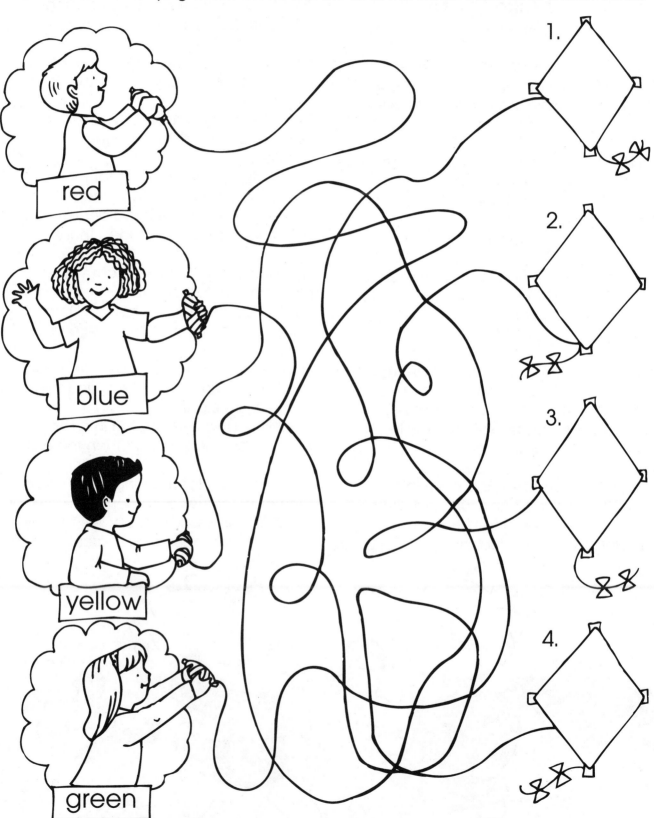

red

blue

yellow

green

1.

2.

3.

4.

Consonant blends
Spring Thing

The word *spring* begins with the consonants *spr*. The three letters work together to form the beginning sound of this word. Many other words you know begin with consonant blends. Draw a line from the correct set of letters to finish each word. Use the pictures as clues.

st   ag

sk   ain

br   og

fr   ead

fl   unk

sp   amp

dr   ess

tr   ider

br   esent

pr   idge

Name _____

Kite Chaos

Look at all of these kites! What words could you use to describe them? You could:

- tell how many with number words, or words like *few*, *several* or *many*
- tell what color they are
- tell about the design
- tell if they are pretty, ugly, cool or . . .?

All of these words are adjectives. Some of the adjectives you could use to describe kites are listed in the word box and hidden in this puzzle. Circle all the words that you find. They may be spelled backwards or forwards going up, down, across or diagonally.

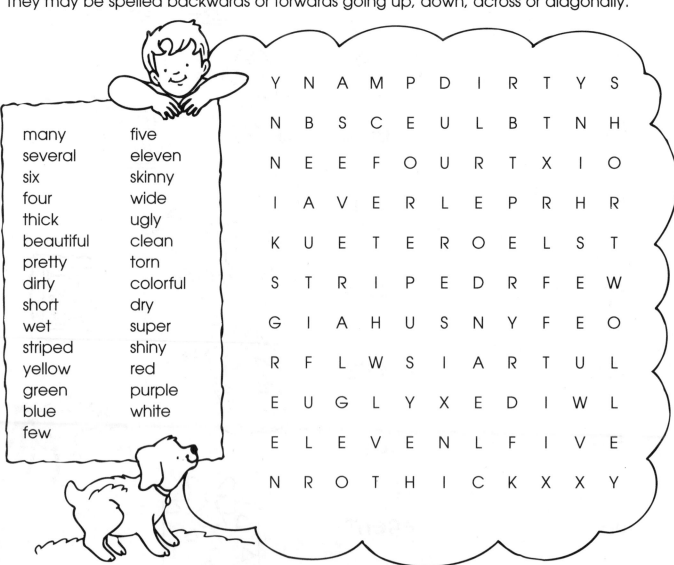

many	five
several	eleven
six	skinny
four	wide
thick	ugly
beautiful	clean
pretty	torn
dirty	colorful
short	dry
wet	super
striped	shiny
yellow	red
green	purple
blue	white
few	

```
Y  N  A  M  P  D  I  R  T  Y  S
N  B  S  C  E  U  L  B  T  N  H
N  E  E  F  O  U  R  T  X  I  O
I  A  V  E  R  L  E  P  R  H  R
K  U  E  T  E  R  O  E  L  S  T
S  T  R  I  P  E  D  R  F  E  W
G  I  A  H  U  S  N  Y  F  E  O
R  F  L  W  S  I  A  R  T  U  L
E  U  G  L  Y  X  E  D  I  W  L
E  L  E  V  E  N  L  F  I  V  E
N  R  O  T  H  I  C  K  X  X  Y
```

On the back, draw a picture of your favorite kite.
Then under the picture, write at least three adjectives to describe your kite.

TLC10408 Copyright © Teaching & Learning Company, Carthage, IL 62321-0010

Name _____

Using context, parts of speech
A Springtime Story

Read the story carefully. Add missing words in each of the blanks, following the directions given. Make your story either serious or silly.

It was the first day of spring. The weather was _____ and
                                                  (adjective)

_____ Andrea was eager to go outside and
(adjective)

_____ , but her mother asked her to _____ first.
(verb)   (verb)

At _____ _____, Andrea's mom told her she could go outside. First
   (time)   (A.M. or P.M.)

Andrea phoned her friend, _____ to see if _____ could join
                          (person's name)   (he or she)

her. Her friend said, "_____. "
                      (Yes or No)

For the rest of the day, _____ had a lot of fun. The best thing
                         (name or names)

that happened was _____
                                      (describe an event)

_____.

Just before she went to bed, Andrea decided that if the weather was

_____ tomorrow, she would like to _____. Her
(adjective)   (verb)

mother thought that was a _____ idea!
                          (adjective)

Now draw a picture to go with your story. Use the back of this page.

Name _____

Springtime Titles

The name of a book is called the title. The first word and all the important words in a title begin with capital letters. The person who wrote the book is called the author. Authors' names begin with capital letters. Initials are capital letters, too. Here are the names of silly books that might be a lot of fun to read in the spring. Circle the letters in the titles that should be capital letters. Write the author's names correctly in the blanks. Do not capitalize these words in titles: a, an, and, for, in, of, on, the, to

1. planting your very first garden, by i. m. dirty _____

_____

2. get help with your outdoor chores, by u. r. needed _____

_____

3. flowers for everyone, by bo kaye_____

4. is it a weed? by paul itout _____

5. allergies in the spring, by hank e. sneeze _____

6. fun things to do with a friend, by letts p. lay _____

_____

7. what do to during a tornado, by stan basement _____

_____

8. how to do your spring cleaning, by s. crub _____

_____

9. have a great yard sale, by price itright_____

10. think now about summer vacation, by plann a. head _____

_____

11. if butterflies could talk, by cy lence _____

12. springtime weather, by april showers _____

Now, on the back of this page, write the title and author of one of your favorite books. Remember to use capital letters.

Name _____

Springtime Babies

In the springtime, many animals give birth to their young. Some animal "babies"
have special names for their young. For example, cats have kittens.
What do dogs have? That's right. They have puppies.

Right the correct name next to each picture. Use the words in this box.

bunny	chick	foal	kid
calf	fawn	lamb	piglet

1. _____

2. _____

3. _____

4. _____

5. _____

6. _____

7. _____

8. _____

Name _____

Tally-Ho!

You can use tally marks to count by fives. Here is how
Mr. Piper is using them to count the packages of seeds in his store:

  = 12 packages
of seeds

卌　　　卌　　　II

Use tally marks to count these packages of seeds.
Write the tally marks under the pictures.

   = _____

_____   _____   _____   _____

Now add the number of tally marks in each box.
Write the correct number in the blank.

卌　II　　　_____	IIII　IIII　IIII　I　　_____
卌 卌 卌 卌　　　_____	卌 卌 卌 卌 IIII　　_____
卌 卌 卌 卌 卌 I　　　_____	卌 卌 卌 卌 卌 卌 IIII　　_____

Name _____

Addition and subtraction facts
Ducklings

These baby ducks, or ducklings, are paddling all over the pond. Some of the mother ducks are having trouble keeping track of their young! Look at this group of ducklings.

The mother duck can use either addition or subtraction to keep track of the ducklings. She knows that she has 14 ducklings altogether. She can use any of these facts:

5 + 9 = 14	14 - 5 = 9
9 + 5 = 14	14 - 9 = 5

Here are more groups of ducklings.
Write four number sentences, like the four above, for each group.

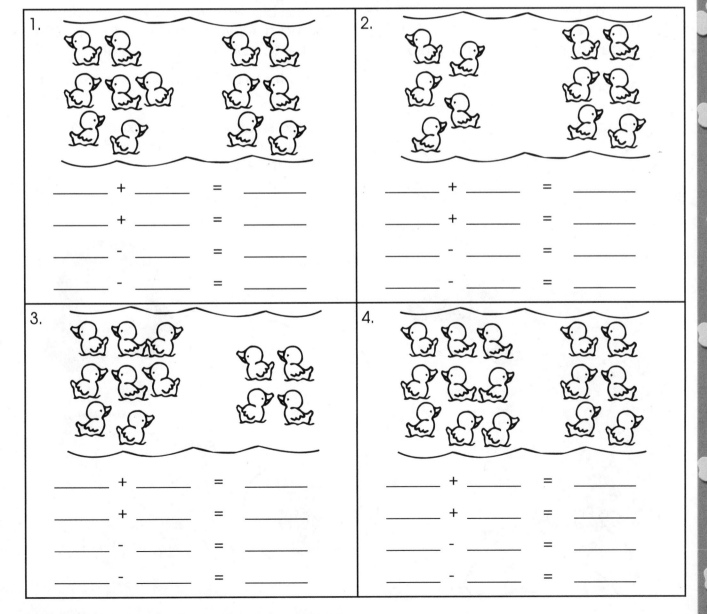

1.

_____ + _____ = _____

_____ + _____ = _____

_____ - _____ = _____

_____ - _____ = _____

2.

_____ + _____ = _____

_____ + _____ = _____

_____ - _____ = _____

_____ - _____ = _____

3.

_____ + _____ = _____

_____ + _____ = _____

_____ - _____ = _____

_____ - _____ = _____

4.

_____ + _____ = _____

_____ + _____ = _____

_____ - _____ = _____

_____ - _____ = _____

National Bubble Week

Have some good clean fun during Naitonal Bubble Week. This national observance is held each year during the week containing the first day of spring. Along with the math and language activities on pages 180-184, you'll also want to have your students just blowing bubbles! There is a lot they can learn from this fun activity.

Here's a basic bubble recipe to get you started:

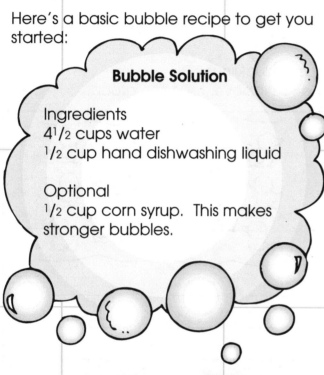

Bubble Solution

Ingredients
4 1/2 cups water
1/2 cup hand dishwashing liquid

Optional
1/2 cup corn syrup. This makes stronger bubbles.

Here are some tips for blowing bigger, better bubbles:

- Make sure your bubble maker, and anything your bubble may touch, is wet.

- Let the bubble maker sit in the soap solution for a few seconds. Do not swish it around in the solution. That creates suds and foam which will break your bubbles.

- As you blow your bubble, finish it with a quick twist of your wrist. This seals the bubble.

- If you get a lot of small bubbles instead of one big one, you may be blowing too hard. Or you may have the bubble maker too close to your mouth.

- Don't try to blow bubbles outside on a windy day.

- Bubble solution can be mixed a few days in advance. The longer it sits, the better it gets.

See pages 178-179 for a science-related activity.

Bubble Wands

How many different devices can you and your students find that work well for blowing bubbles? Here is a list to help you get started:

- drinking straws
- coat hangers, bent into a circular shape
- pipe cleaners or florist wire bent into circles and taped with Scotch™ tape or duct tape
- plastic kitchen funnel
- key rings
- paper towel tube

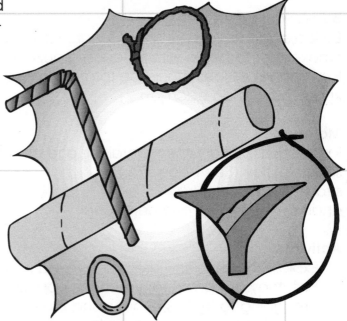

Song
Pop! Goes the Bubble!

To the tune of "Pop Goes the Weasel"

All around the neighborhood*
We like to blow our bubbles
But when a bubble hits the ground*,
Pop goes the bubble!

*Substitute one of these phrases for *the neighborhood* to make additional verses:
my grandmother's house
our play-ay-ground
the u-u-ni-verse
and many other places your students can name.

*Substitute one of these phrases for *the ground* to make additional verses:
my foot
your nose
a tree
and many more your students can add.

Name _____

What Colors Do You See?

Before You Begin

Divide students into groups of four to six students each. Appoint a recordkeeper and timekeeper to begin with for each group. All others should be the bubble blowers. Explain that all jobs should be rotated throughout the activity. Be sure each student knows how to do each job.

Materials

large bowl, pail or other container, one per group
soap solution (See page 176.)
straws
chart on page 179, one per group

Activity

1. Explain that students are going to learn about two different facts regarding bubbles. First, they are going to watch their bubbles to see what colors appear. Secondly, they are going to try to see how long they can make their bubbles last. First, use solution without the corn syrup. In order to keep track of information, the blowers should all blow one bubble at the same time while the recorder and the timekeeper do their jobs.

2. Instruct the blowers in each group to dip their straws into the dish of solution. When the timekeeper says, "Go," they should gently blow through their straws. Tell them to pay close attention to the colors they see in their bubbles. They should call out the colors that they see while the recordkeeper marks them on the chart.

3. At the same time, the timekeeper should watch the time and notice how long the longest bubble lasts. He should call the time out to the recordkeeper who then writes it at the bottom of the chart.

4. After everyone has had the same job for two rounds, students should switch jobs and repeat several more rounds.

5. Repeat steps 1-4 above using solution with corn syrup. If possible, try to do at least 10 rounds both with and without the syrup.

Wrap Up

Bring the groups together and compare findings. Did students see all the colors of the spectrum? (They should!) Did they find that bubbles with corn syrup last longer than ones without? Why do they think the bubbles always rise? (The warm air from the blower's lungs causes it to rise.) Before you leave this activity, you may want students to make graphs with the information in their charts.

Name _____

Bubble Log

The recordkeeper should put an X under each blower's name next to the colors that person sees in his or her bubble. You may put more than one X in each box.

Colors Seen by Bubble Blowers

Name of bubble → blower					
red					
orange					
yellow					
blue					
indigo					
blue-violet					

Length of Time for Longest Bubble for Each Round

Without corn syrup   With corn syrup

Round 1		Round 6		Round 1		Round 6	
Round 2		Round 7		Round 2		Round 7	
Round 3		Round 8		Round 3		Round 8	
Round 4		Round 9		Round 4		Round 9	
Round 5		Round 10		Round 5		Round 10	

Counting circles

How Many Bubbles?

Look at Brock! He is having fun blowing a lot of bubbles.
Count the number of bubbles that you find. Write the number in the blank.

Name _____

Bubble Tales

Pretend you've just been given these five magic bubbles. One at a time, you pop them. What comes out of the bubble? Use your imagination to find out. Finish the sentence inside each bubble. Then draw a picture to go with your story on the back of this page.

1.
In my first magic bubble, I just knew I would find a very special friend. And I was right, I popped it and I found _____.
I was very happy because

_____

_____

_____.

2.
Next, I hoped to find a special animal. When I popped my bubble I found

_____

_____

_____

_____

_____.

3.
My next bubble was a magical book called

_____.

It told the story of _____

_____

_____

_____

_____.

4.
My fourth bubble was the chance to give the best gift ever! I decided to give _____

to _____

because _____

_____

_____.

5.
For my last bubble, I had to _____

_____.

Instead I found a trip to _____

_____

_____!

I was very _____

_____.

Name _____

The Shape of a Bubble

How would you describe the shape of a bubble? You might say it is round, and that is right! But is it round in the same way that a paper plate is round? No, because a paper plate is flat and a bubble is not.

The correct name for the shape of a bubble is a sphere. We say that it is a shape that has volume, because you could hold something inside of it. What is being held inside a bubble? That's right, it's air. Think about a softball. It, too, has volume. It is filled with string. You could also think that the softball is able to hold water. A paper plate is not able to hold water, is it?

Think about the objects below. The ones that are round and flat are simply called circles. Draw a ring around the shapes that are circles. The ones that are round and could contain air, water or some other substance, are spheres. Draw a line under the spheres. Some of the things shown here are neither circles nor spheres. Put an X on these shapes.

Name _____

Bubble Math 1

Cut out the bubble numbers at the bottom of the page. Then move them around in different spots in the problems below. Find a way to use every number just one time. When you find a solution that works, paste the numbers on your page.

1. ◯
  + ◯
  ——
  5

2. ◯
  + ◯
  ——
  8

3. ◯
  + ◯
  ——
  9

4. ◯
  + ◯
  ——
  10

5. ◯
  + ◯
  ——
  13

⓪	②	④	⑥	⑧
①	③	⑤	⑦	⑨

TLC10408 Copyright © Teaching & Learning Company, Carthage, IL 62321-0010

Name _____

Bubble Math 2

Cut out the bubble numbers at the bottom of the page. Place them in the
puzzle so that the three numbers in every row total 15.
When you find an answer that works, paste your numbers onto your page.

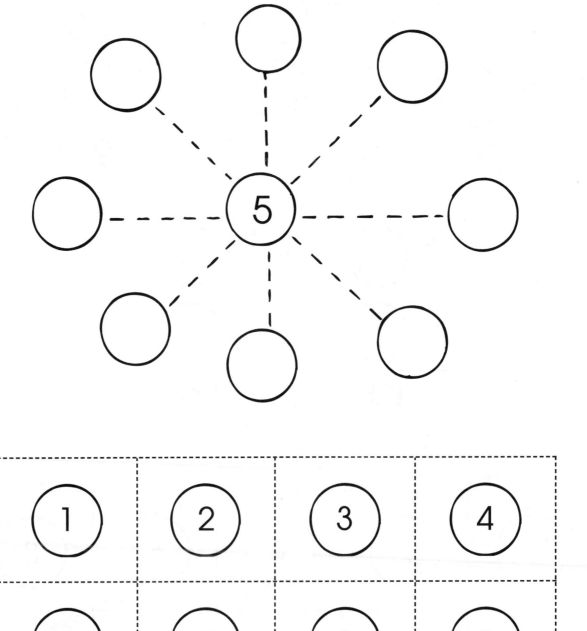

184

April

Get ready for an amazing April! Here is a fresh assortment of bulletin boards, teacher helps and curriculum reproducible pages to see you through many of the special days in April.

We've chosen six special themes: National Poetry Month, Keep America Beautiful Month, April Fools' Day, National Library Week, Be Kind to Animals Week and Easter. For some themes you will find a bulletin board, a song or a resource list. For all of the units you will have appealing reproducibles that cover important spring-time skills. Most skill sheets are for math, language and general thinking skills.

Pick the themes you are most interested in and select activities and worksheets that are on an appropriate level for your students. You will be able to use many ideas in each unit even though some individual pages may be too difficult or too simple for your particular class.

First your students will listen, read and write poetry for National Poetry Month. On these pages you'll find teacher resource pages with tips for student poems, a shape book pattern and a bulletin board idea. There are are also reproducibles that help students brush up on skills with rhyming words, addition and pie graphs.

"Keep America Beautiful" is the theme of the second section, which is also suitable for Earth Day on April 22. Activity ideas are included, along with more skill sheets for rhyming words, opposites, addition, measurements and more. Another bulletin board idea can be found here as well.

Jokes and humor are the core of the April Fools' Day section on pages 211-220. These pages are also appropriate for the wider theme of National Humor Month in April. Students can make their own joke books, contribute to a joke-filled bulletin board, read an April Fools' Day story, solve a logic puzzle and more.

National Library Week is a marvelous observance to celebrate with your young students. After your students solve a maze and try to count the number of books in your library, they can write a thank-you note to the librarian with the form provided.

Be Kind to Animals Week and Easter round out the themes in this resource. Review consonant sounds, capitalization and writing sentences. Be sure to use the pet shop math page for some extra fun with addition and estimation.

Don't forget all the great bonus clip art on the CD! It promises to make for a truly amazing April in your classroom!

National Poetry Month

Share the joy of poems, songs and rhyming words during National Poetry Month this April. See page 189 for a list of just a few of the great children's poetry books that are available. You'll want to read many of these and other books to your students. While we know that poems do not have to be made of rhyming words, many of the famous, fun poems for children do rhyme. Consider the many books by Dr. Seuss and the popular nursery rhymes, such as "Hickory, Dickory, Dock."

Ideas for Using Published Poetry

• Read a well-known nursery rhyme such as "Hey, Diddle, Diddle." Ask students to picture a barnyard scene where a cat is playing a fiddle and a cow is actually jumping sky-high. Then ask them to speculate about the other nonsense that could be happening with other animals. What would a horse, sheep, goat or pig be doing that could be funny? Put students in small groups to write a new nursery rhyme, modeled after one that they know.

• Tell students that you are going to read four different poems to them. They should listen closely and then decide which one they like best. Then read and discuss the poems. Ask students to vote, and tally the results. (See page 196.) If desired, group students according to their favorite poems. If appropriate, give each group a copy of their chosen poem. Ask the group to practice reading their poem aloud together, and then have them read it to the entire class. Or, ask each group to make up actions or a fingerplay to go with their poem.

• Use a short poem for handwriting practice. Write it neatly on the chalkboard or overhead and ask students to copy it in their best handwriting. They may wish to frame their poem and add illustrations.

Ideas for Writing Non-Rhyming Poetry

• Construct visual poems. Give children the fun of creating visual pictures with single words. Consider these examples:

TALL _{small}

Let students choose a word that they can picture. Here are a few ideas: *apple, snake, motorcycle, circle, elephant, giraffe, tree.*

- Brainstorm together on a specific image. For example, ask the question, "What is spring?" Have the students respond with as many words or phrases as they can make up. Record all responses on the chalkboard. For the first experience, compile a few of the responses into a free verse like this:

What Is Spring?

Spring is a time
    for flying kites.
Spring is a time
    for eating ice cream cones.
Spring is a time
    for riding bikes.
Spring is a time
    for laughter.

Other possible brainstorming topics include vacation, family, eagles, friends, rain and so on.

- Imagine together what it would be like to . . .
  be one-inch tall looking at the world
  be an ant tunneling down an anthill
  be a rose opening itself to the morning sun
  or many other fantasy situations.

Again record students' responses as you work together as a class or in small groups.

- Write ABC poetry. Choose one letter of the alphabet to begin. Write a line using that letter and several of the letters that follow it. Here are two examples:

Frank
Gave
Henry
Italian
Jelly.

Porcupines, so very
Quietly,
Ran around the
Sandy seashore.

- Write acrostics. This is similar to the ABC poetry. In acrostics, the first letters of lines spell out the title to the poem. It is a bit tricky, but possible, with young students if short words are chosen. Here are two examples:

Feeling my way
Outside in a cloud, I am
Glad for the streetlights.

Shining
Until
Noon.

Other short words to use include *wind, cat, dog, home, work, bug, ant, bee, sky, farm, bird,* etc.

Ideas for Writing Rhyming Poetry

One of the basic building blocks of rhymed verse is the *couplet*, a simple two lines
of verse that end with the same sounds:

> I like to watch the busy bees
> Fly all around the maple trees.

- Use the bulletin board idea shown on page 190 to collect rhyming words. Challenge students to use a word pair and build it into a couplet. Encourage them to keep adding word pairs to the display all through the month.

- Another way to help students write rhymed verse is to supply the first line for them. Choose your line so that it ends with a word that is easily rhymed. Ask the students to copy your line and add one of their own. Here are a few sample opening lines:
  Jason found a big gray cat . . .
  At the bottom of the deep, blue sea . . .
  I like to fly my very own kite . . .
  Easter eggs and chocolate candy . . .
  Poor little Sarah had nothing to do . . .
  Let's go play and have some fun . . .

- When students are comfortable with couplets, you may want to challenge them to write longer rhymed verses with pairs of couplets, or poems with other rhyme schemes.

Young students may be able to orally complete couplets and other rhymed poems that they are not yet able to write. If possible, have older students or adult volunteers available to write down the poems that these children create.

While children of all ages will enjoy listening to clever limericks, do not expect primary students to write these and other highly structured forms of poetry with limits on syllable counts, overall length, etc. Since students of this age are able to enjoy listening to many great poems in a variety of forms, please, read, read, read to your students!

Resources

Animal Trunk: Silly Poems to Read Aloud, Charles Ghigna Gabriel (Illustrator). Harry N. Abrams, Inc., 1999.

Favorite Poems for Children by Holly Pell McConnaughy. Barnes & Noble Books, 1993.

The Frogs Wore Red Suspenders by Jack Prelutsky.
Book: Greenwillow Books, 2002.
Audio: ISBN: 0060012447, HarperCollins Publishers, 2002.

Hop on Pop by Dr. Seuss. Random House, Inc., 1976.

It's Raining Pigs and Noodles by Jack Prelutsky. HarperCollins Children's Books, 2000.

Never Take a Pig to Lunch: Poems About the Fun of Eating by Nadine Bernard Westcott, Editor. Orchard Books, 1994.

The Original Mother Goose by Blanche Fisher Wright, Running Press Book Publishers, 1992.

Tie Your Socks and Clap Your Feet: Mixed-Up Poems by Lenny Hort. Simon & Schuster Children's, 1999.

Tortillitas Para Mama: And Other Nursery Rhymes, Spanish and English by Margot C. Griego, et al. Econo-Clad Books, 1987.

Walking the Bridge of Your Nose: Wordplay Poems Rhymes by Michael Rosen. Kingfisher, 1999.

What If?: Just Wondering Poems by Joy N. Hulme. Boyds Mills Press, 1993.

Where the Sidewalk Ends by Shel Silverstein. 25th Anniversary Edition. HarperCollins Children's Books, 2000.

National Poetry Month

April's the time to make a rhyme!

				1 cat mat	2 me be
3 rain plain	4	5 hand band	6	7 hair bear	8	9
10	11 book hook	12	13 bird word	14 snake lake	15	16 dog log
17 mouse house	18	19 tea three car star	20	21 fish dish	22 cat rat lie fly	23
24 hen pen	25 red bed	26 pear fair	27 zoo blue	28 sun fun ant plant	29 rug bug	30

April is National Poetry Month.

Encourage students to write pairs of rhyming words on the calendar pages. They may write them on the day that they find the words, or on any empty day on the page. If they write small enough, they will have space for oodles of words!

Shape Book Pattern

Name _____

Identifying rhyming words

Match Game

Find a picture on the left that matches a picture on the right.
Draw lines to match the rhyming words.

Writing rhyming sentences
Comic Strip

Here is part of a comic strip. Can you finish it? First, think of a way to finish each sentence so that the last word of the sentence rhymes with the last word that's already printed in the first sentence in each box. Then draw a picture in each box to go with the sentences.

1. Sally found her friend Billy.

   She thought he looked very _____!

2. He wore a hat that came from a clown,

   And his big red nose was upside- _____.

3. Billy pulled a rabbit from a hat.

   He said, "Now, Sally, can you do_____?"

4. Sally smiled and gave it her best try.

   But out of the hat instead came a _____!

Name _____

Oral reading poem
Up in the Sky
by Ann Richmond Fisher

High up in the sky
I see an apple pie!

Down below the ground
I see a chocolate mound.

Along the winding stream
I see some cold ice cream.

Out on the quiet lake
I see a two-tiered cake.

By the big, wide road
I see pie a la' mode.

'Way up in the mountain
I see a soda fountain.

Along the many bustling streets
I see some fancy, tasty sweets.

And if I walk or ride a bike
I always find a food I like.

So tell me, won't you please, my friend,
When will this problem ever end?

When I look high up in the sky
And all I see is apple pie,
It makes me think I need to try
To have a doctor check my eyes!

Poetic Math

Name _____

Do you know the name of one of the most popular rhyming children's story?
You will find the title and author when you complete this page.
Solve each addition problem. Then write the letter that matches each sum. Read the
words that you spell to find the title and author. The first one is done for you.

```
  6     5     6        4     9     7        2     5       | 9  = C
  4     3     0        4     8     4        5     3       | 10 = N
+ 5   + 10  + 6      + 1   + 3   + 4      + 6   + 2       | 11 = Y
 ___   ___   ___      ___   ___   ___      ___   ___      | 12 = E
  15                                                      | 13 = I
                                                          | 14 = U
  T                                                       | 15 = T
                                                          | 16 = D
                                                          | 17 = B
  4     9     3        5     6     6        9     4       | 18 = H
  7     9     5        7     9     7        4     5       | 19 = S
+ 4   + 0   + 4      + 6   + 5   + 2      + 4   + 2       | 20 = A
 ___   ___   ___      ___   ___   ___      ___   ___      | 21 = R


  5     8       10    4     4     7     5
  4     5        4    4     7     6     7
+ 7   + 8      + 5   + 4   + 3   + 6   + 7
 ___   ___      ___   ___   ___   ___   ___
```

Name _____

Reading a circle graph
Pie Poems

Mrs. Rhyme's second grade students voted on their favorite poems.
They could choose between these titles:

Jabberwocky by Lewis Carroll
White Sheep, White Sheep by Christina Rossetti
From a Railway Carriage by Robert Louis Stevenson
One Fish, Two Fish by Dr. Seuss

This pie graph shows how the students voted.

Favorite Poems of Second Graders

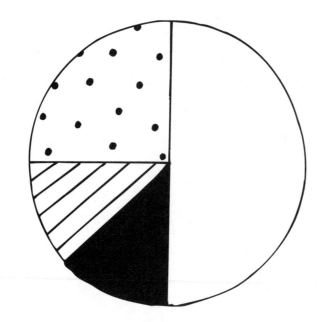

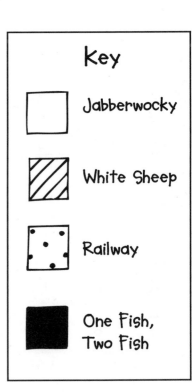

Key

☐ Jabberwocky

▨ White Sheep

▦ Railway

■ One Fish, Two Fish

Circle the correct answer.

1. Which poem was chosen the most?

   Jabberwocky   White Sheep   Railway   One Fish, Two Fish

2. Which poem received the second highest number of votes?

   Jabberwocky   White Sheep   Railway   One Fish, Two Fish

3. What two poems received an equal number of votes?

   White Sheep & Railway   Railway & One Fish   White Sheep & One Fish

Hold a vote in your classroom for four or five good poems. Make a graph of the results.

Keep America Beautiful Month

April is Keep America Beautiful Month, and April 22 is Earth Day. What better time to clean up the playground and talk about recycling? You can get your primary students into the swing of things by teaching them the song on page 200.

Discussion questions to use during April:

• What natural beauty do you see in America?

• What are your favorite beautiful things to see here?

• Tell us about the most beautiful park you've ever visited.

• How do people spoil the beauty of our parks and playgrounds?

• What can each of us do to keep our own playground and neighborhood beautiful?

• Why does recycling help to keep our country beautiful?

• What things can be recycled at a local recycling center?

• What things can you simply reuse at home and at school?

Activity Ideas

• Bring several paper grocery sacks to school. Show them to the class and brainstorm possible ways the sacks can be reused. Ideas include: costumes, puppets, gift wrap, waste can liners, etc. Do the same with plastic shopping bags and milk jugs.

• Take a walk around the playground on a nice day and pick up litter that you find. Caution: Be sure children do not handle sharp or unsafe items. Be sure they wash their hands with soap and warm water as soon as they return to the building.

• Visit a recycling center. Learn how paper, aluminum or plastic is reused.

• Take a nature walk in a wooded area. Instruct students ahead of time that they are not to pick wildflowers, harm animal homes or leave any litter behind them. Point out the different kinds of plants, insects and animals. Enjoy nature!

• Place a bird feeder outside a classroom window. Here's one simple way to do it: Cut a grapefruit or orange in half. Scoop out the fruit and use the empty skin for a feeder. Fill the feeder halfway with suet and birdseed. Place the feeder in the crook of a tree branch. Try to identify the birds that you see. Start a list of the birds that come to eat at your feeder. Check the feeder often and keep it full.

• Start adding your own beauty to your surroundings. Plant flower seeds (marigolds or zinnias work well) in small disposable cups. Keep them indoors by a window. When the danger of frost is past, and the seedlings are large enough to separate, plant them outdoors, either in a corner of the school yard or at home.

Keep America Beautiful Month

Put litter in its place . . . .

and keep America beautiful!

Use the pattern on page 199 for the trash can. Enlarge it, if necessary, and copy it onto gray paper. Staple bits of real trash onto the board. Crumpled lunch bags, candy wrappers, Styrofoam™ cups and more can be attached to your board. If you like, you can staple crumpled newspaper behind the trash can as you attach it to make it look padded or stuffed. Attach stars for an extra patriotic touch!

Name _____

Teacher: You may adapt these verses or suggest that students write more of their own.
Notice that the verses here do not use rhyming lines.

Song
Oh the Litter!

To the tune of "Clementine"

Chorus
Oh the litter,
Oh the litter,
Oh the litter in our land!
We will bend and pick it up
Oh the litter in our land!

Verse 1
On the playground at our school
There's a broken bicycle.
We should take it home and fix it
So our playground will be clean.

Verse 2
At a campground in a park
There's a pile of old pop cans.
We should take them to recycling
So our campground will be clean.

Verse 3
In our backyard by the alley
Someone left a broken chair
We should give it to the trashman
So our backyard will be clean.

Verse 4
All across our neighborhood
There are papers, cups and cans.
We should always pick up litter
To keep our country beautiful.

Final Chorus
Oh the beauty,
Oh the beauty,
Oh the beauty in our land!
We have picked up all the litter,
Oh the beauty in our land!

Name _____

Lots of Litter

Oh, no! Look at all this litter! Marco and Maria were hoping to enjoy a picnic with their family, but when they arrived at the park, they found this mess.
Begin by putting an X on every item that does not belong in the park. Then cut out parts of the picture that do belong in the park. Glue them on to a new sheet of paper. Add more drawings of your own, and color your picture.

TLC10408 Copyright © Teaching & Learning Company, Carthage, IL 62321-0010

Name _____

Bicycle Built for Two

Nate and his Dad are sharing a bicycle built for two. They are enjoying the beauty of nature as they ride through the park. At first these two pictures look alike, but check again! Find six things in the top picture that are missing from the bottom picture. Circle them in the top picture, and try to draw them in the bottom one.

Name _____

Trash Can Families

What is a trash can family? It's a group of words that belong together because the words all end with the same sound. Look at the first trash can. It contains five words that all rhyme with *trash*. Can you read all the words in that trash can?

Look at the rest of the trash cans. In each can, add three more words that are in the same family. Notice that not all rhyming words are spelled with the same letters. In trash can #3, for example, one word ends in *eak* and the other one ends in *ake*. But words still rhyme.

1. trash
   cash

   mash

   rash

   flash

2. can
   plan

3. break
   stake

4. that
   rat

5. wing
   string

6. stand
   land

7. think
   pink

8. bean
   queen

9. train
   mane

Opposites, spelling

America the Beautiful

During Keep America Beautiful Month, it's a good time to think about opposites.
Lots of litter can change a beautiful playground into an ugly one.
If something is not clean, it is probably dirty. Read each word below.
Then unscramble the letters next to it to spell its opposite.

Example: hot—dolc <u>cold</u>

1. sad—payhp _____

2. old—goyun _____

3. long—thors _____

4. awake—lepase _____

5. far—aren _____

6. few—yamn _____

7. all—oenn _____

8. always—veenr _____

9. slow—ciukq _____

10. sit—natsd _____

11. tiny—grela _____

12. dark—gilht _____

13. arrive—valee _____

14. left—thigr _____

15. over—drenu _____

Using context to supply missing words

Nature Walk

The story below is missing several words. Use the meaning of the words in the story to figure out which words are missing. Write a word from the word box in each blank.

Mr. Tyler's _____ went on a nature walk. First they walked through the playground. Then they crossed the _____. Finally, the students began walking on a ____ in the woods.

"Tell me what you see," said Mr. Tyler.

"I see a tall ____ tree," reported Bryce.

"____! There's a butterfly!" exclaimed Betsy.

"I see three baby ____ in a nest in that tree," said Amy.

There were so many beautiful things to see in the woods. Steve saw some ____ wildflowers. Kelsie saw some wiggly ____. Kyle thought he saw a ____ running across the ground. Rob noticed a maple tree with tiny new ____.

At the end of their walk, Mr. Tyler asked a tricky _____. "What didn't you see?" he asked. "It's something I was hoping we would *not* see, and we didn't!"

The students thought and thought. At last Rob raised his ____.

"I know, Mr. Tyler! We didn't see any ____!" he shouted.

All at once, everyone knew Rob was ____. Everyone cheered.

pine	leaves	street	look	question	trail	purple
class	hand	right	worms	gopher	litter	robins

Using approximate units of measurement
Best Guess

Look at these containers that you might gather for recycling or trash collecting.
Think about how much each one holds. Circle the better estimate.

1.

a. 12 ounces

b. 12 pounds

2.

a. 1 cup

b. 1 gallon

3.

a. 32 cups

b. 32 gallons

4.

a. 30 ounces

b. 30 pounds

5.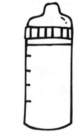

a. 1 cup

b. 1 gallon

6.

a. 2 cups

b. 2 gallons

7.

a. 46 ounces

b. 46 pounds

8.

a. 1 cup

b. 1 gallon

9.

a. 5 ounces

b. 5 pounds

Name _____

Addition of two-digit numbers
Garbage Trucks

These four garbage trucks are driven by Jed, Ned, Ted and Redd. Which driver will pick up the most trash? On each path there are numbers that show how many trash cans each driver will empty along his route. Add the numbers in each path. Write the sums in the blanks at the end of the paths. Circle the name of the driver who picks up the most. Color the two trucks with the same totals.

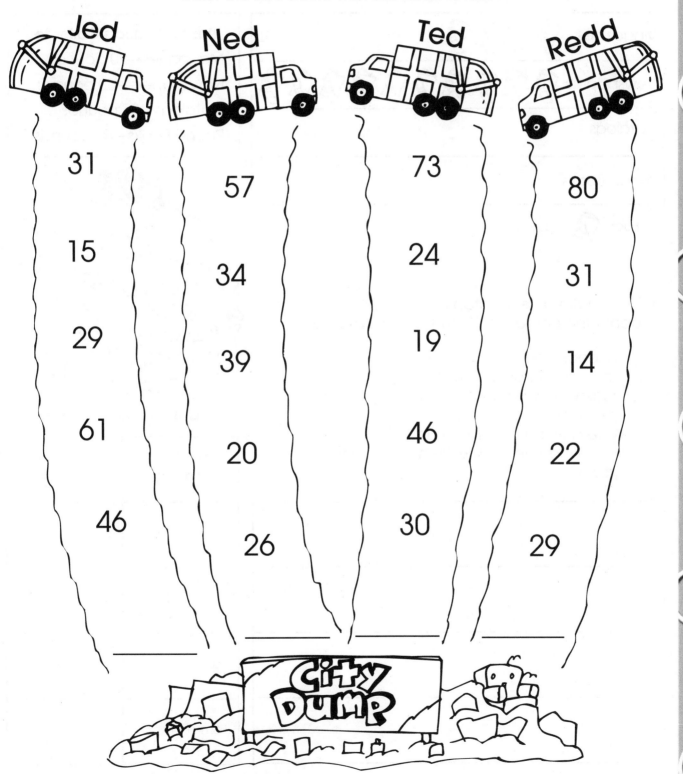

Jed

31

15

29

61

46

_____

Ned

57

34

39

20

26

_____

Ted

73

24

19

46

30

_____

Redd

80

31

14

22

29

_____

City Dump

Name _____

Recycled Graph

A. This chart shows the amount of paper products that were collected in Keith's class. Finish the pictograph below to show the same information.

Paper Products Collected

Magazines	
Newspapers	
Catalogs	
Phone Books	

Each  = 5 pounds.

Paper Products Collected

Magazines—20 pounds
Newspapers—50 pounds
Catalogs—35 pounds
Phone Books—40 pounds

B. Now make a new pictograph for this information about the containers Keith's class collected.

1. List each item.
2. Choose your own picture.
3. Decide how many containers are equal to one picture.
4. Write a title above the graph.
5. Write what the picture means below the graph.

Containers Collected

Types of Container	Number Collected
Aluminum	60
Glass	40
Large plastic	30
Small plastic	50

Name _____

Rosa's Route

Rosa is traveling to different schools in her county, teaching about how to "Keep America Beautiful." Look at the map of Green County. Then answer the questions below.

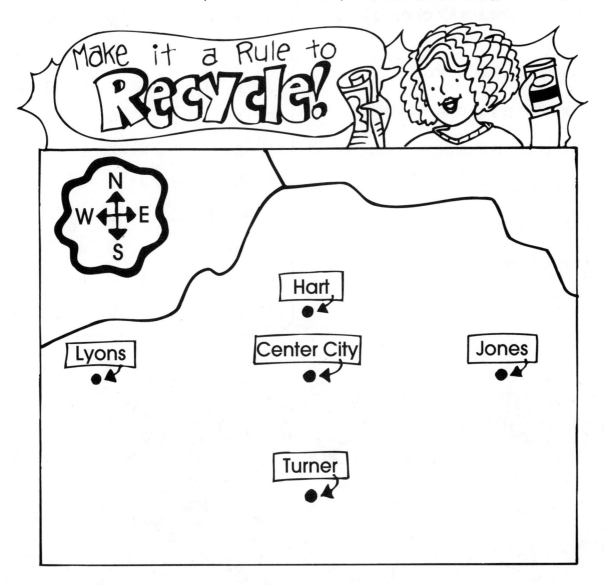

1. Rosa starts her day in Center City. What town is closest to her? _____
2. If Rosa drives straight east from Center City, in what city will she arrive? _____
3. What city is north of Center City? _____
4. In what direction should Rosa travel to go from Center City to Turner?

      north   south   east   west

5. In what direction should Rosa travel to go from Lyons to Jones?

      north   south   east   west

6. In what direction should Rosa travel to go from Turner to Hart?

      north   south   east   west

Solving a word search

Earth Search

Look at the word search. Try to find words about the Earth. Circle the words that you find. Use the pictures for clues to these words:

1. Find three weather words.

2. Find four things you can recycle.

3. Find three things that grow in the ground.

4. Find one kind of bird.

5. Find two insects.

6. Find three kinds of baby animals.

S	R	E	P	A	P	S	W	E	N
G	Z	O	W	I	N	D	Y	X	Q
U	G	K	B	E	E	J	K	B	S
J	L	I	U	I	F	Q	R	N	P
C	A	T	T	Y	N	I	A	R	Y
I	S	T	T	X	Z	C	S	O	N
T	S	E	E	R	T	L	D	G	N
S	H	N	R	Y	U	Z	E	W	U
A	B	S	F	L	O	W	E	R	S
L	K	J	L	A	M	B	S	D	Z
P	Y	W	Y	S	E	V	L	A	C

April Fools' Day

This section of activities may be used on April 1 for April Fools' Day, or all month long for National Humor Month. While learning about tricks and jokes may not seem like learning at all, it can be a great time for students to practice their handwriting, read high-interest material and learn important social skills. Students will probably not even mind the reading and writing practice when they are having so much fun laughing!

When discussing April Fools' Day, explain that on April first many people enjoy telling jokes and playing tricks on each other. Some tricks are really funny and are harmless. Other tricks can be mean and hurtful. Here are some examples of April Fools' Day tricks. Read them to your students and ask them if they think they are funny or mean.

- Susie stuffed newspaper in the toe of her dad's workboots last night. In the morning, he tries to put on his boots and realizes they don't fit.

- Ramie put salt in the sugar bowl last night. In the morning, his mom puts a spoonful of it in her coffee.

Students may see that placing salt in the sugar bowl will ruin one cup of coffee. They may or may not decide that is harmful. Stuffing newspaper in the toe of a boot is relatively harmless.

Focus on some fun jokes with the bulletin board on pages 212-213. Ask students to select a joke that they think their classmates would enjoy, and one that they may not already know. (You may wish to give them advance notice and allow them time to ask for their family's help in selecting one.)

Next, photocopy pages 215-216 for students to use in making their own joke booklets. Fold the pages as directed, and put them together like this to form a booklet.

Encourage students to take the booklets home and complete the pages with their families. Many of the pages can be colored, too. Use the jokes on page 212 to help your students get started on their own collections.

Enjoy the other curriculum pages in this unit as well. Don't miss the listening comprehension lesson, the logic puzzle and the math activities on pages 217-220.

Jokes

Animal Jokes

Q: How do you paint a rabbit?
A: With harespray!

Q: What is a mouse's favorite dessert?
A: Cheesecake!

Q: What's green and jumps a foot every three seconds?
A: A frog with hiccups!

Riddles

Q: What do police officers put on their peanut butter sandwiches?
A: Traffic jams!

Q: What color is rain?
A: Water color!

Q: What did the baby corn say to its mother?
A: Where's "pop"corn?

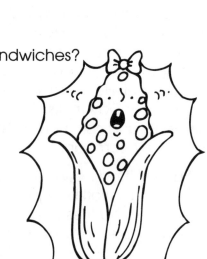

Knock-Knock Jokes

Knock, knock.
    Who's there?
Soup.
    Soup, who?
Superman!

Knock, knock.
    Who's there?
Ida.
    Ida, who?
I'd appreciate it if you would open the door!

Knock, knock.
    Who's there?
Twig.
    Twig, who?
Twig or tweet!

April Fools' Day

Use the pattern on page 214 for the center of the display. Using a circle, square or rectangle of bright construction paper, students should write down a favorite joke, sign it and add it to the bulletin board. If it's a question-and-answer joke, they can write the answer on the back. Use this occasion to emphasize the importance of good handwriting. Instruct students to write as neatly as possible so that their classmates can enjoy their joke.

Name _____

Joke Book
See page 211 for directions.

_____
_____
_____
_____
_____
_____
_____
_____

My favorite knock-knock joke!

_____

This joke book belongs to:

Circle all the silly things in this picture.

MEOW.

Ha Ha Tee-Hee

My Very Own Joke Book

_____

_____

_____

_____

_____

_____

_____

_____

My favorite riddle!

A picture to go
with my animal joke.

A picture about my riddle.

My favorite animal joke!

_____

_____

_____

_____

_____

_____

_____

Name _____

Trick the Teacher

Read this story aloud to your class. Then ask your students to answer the
questions aloud at the bottom of the page. Alternately, you may wish to
reproduce the story and ask each child to read it for himself.
Write the questions on the board, and ask each student to write out her answers.

Trick the Teacher?

It was April Fools' Day. The students in Mr. Smith's class were excited about playing a trick on their teacher. He loved to tell jokes, and they were sure he would laugh when their joke was played on him.

The students had decided they would change places with each other and sit in the wrong places. He would be surprised when he saw Sarah sitting in Trent's seat and Ronnie sitting at the teacher's desk!

It was almost time for school to start. Mr. Smith had not come into the classroom yet. All the students quickly hurried around the room into the wrong seat. At last they were all set.

"I hope Mr. Smith is really surprised!" said Sarah.

"I hope so, too," said the rest of the class.

Just then the door opened, and into the classroom walked Mrs. Short, the art teacher.

"I'm sorry, class, but Mr. Smith is ill today, and the principal asked me to take his place."

"Oh! That's too bad," Ronnie said, "because were going to play an April Fools' trick on him."

"Yes," added Trent. "We had this all planned. I am sorry that Mr. Smith is not here!" And the rest of the class agreed.

"Well," replied Mrs. Short, "I guess he tricked you first!"

And in walked Mr. Smith with a great big grin on his face.

1. Why was Mr. Smith smiling at the end of the story?

   _____

2. Why was Mrs. Short in the class?

   _____

3. Who was going to sit in the teacher's chair?

   _____

4. Was the trick by the kids a good trick or a bad trick? Why? Was the trick by
   Mr. Smith a good trick or a bad trick? Why?

   _____

5. How do you think the students felt at the very end of the story?

   _____

Name _____

Tricky Students

Three friends, Leo, Nick and Jana, played tricks on April Fools' Day.
Here are the tricks they played:
One child tied his classmate's shoestrings to his desk.
One child hid the teacher's math book.
One child put his or her own lunch in a friend's lunch bag.

Read the clues to decide who played which trick.

Clues

1. Jana doesn't know how to tie shoestrings.

2. A boy hid the teacher's math book.

3. Leo did not hide the math book.

Answers

A. _____ tied his or her classmate's shoestrings to the desk.

B. _____ hid the teacher's math book.

C. _____ put his or her own lunch in a friend's lunch bag.

Now draw a picture of a good trick you might play on someone.

Number recognition, numbers
Dots Not Right!

Someone made these dominoes just for April Fools' Day! You can see that for many of the dominoes, the number on the tiles do not match the number of dots. Circle the dominoes with the correct number. Cross out the tiles with the wrong number.

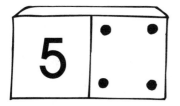 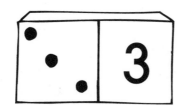 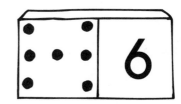

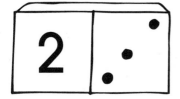 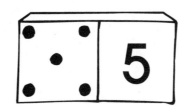 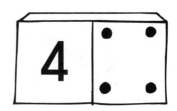

Write the correct number on these tiles.

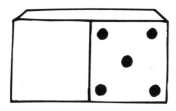 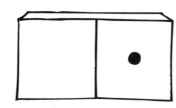 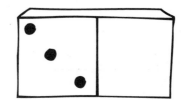

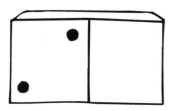 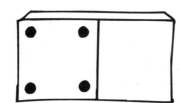 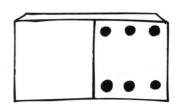

Draw the correct number of dots on these tiles.

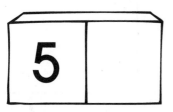 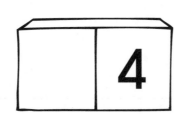 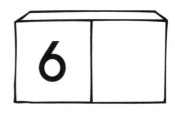

Name _____

Teacher: Ask students to measure the labeled lines in centimeters if you wish to avoid fractional parts of inches.

Optical illusions, measuring

The Long Way

In each picture, try to find the longest line. Is it A, B or C? Write the letter of your guess. Then measure the lines with your ruler. Write the letter for your answer after you measure.

1. Guess _____   Measure _____

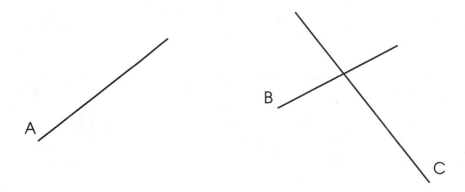

2. Guess _____   Measure _____

  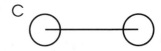

3. Guess _____   Measure _____

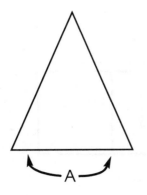 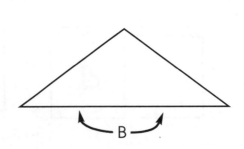 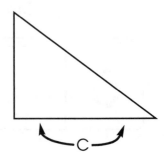

National Library Week

National Library Week is observed in early April. There are also many other literature-related observances in this month of interest to young readers:

- April 2—International Children's Book Day

- April 2—Birthday of Hans Christian Andersen (1805-1875), author of *The Ugly Duckling, The Snow Queen* and many other children's stories

- April 3—Birthday of Washington Irving (1783-1859), author of *Rip Van Winkle, The Legend of Sleepy Hollow* and more.

- A day during the first week of April - Thank You School Librarian Day

- April 9—Anniversary of the first American public library, opened in New Hampshire in 1833.

- April 12—Birthday of Beverly Cleary (1916-), author of *Ramona the Pest, Dear Mr. Henshaw* and more.

- April 27—Birthday of Ludwig Bemelmans (1898-1962), author of the *Madeline* books.

Take your students to the library often during April (and every month!). Help them to see that libraries are where a million journeys into the wonderful world of literature begin. Teach them the skills needed to make the most of the library in your school. Be sure to reserve a time when you or your librarian can teach the entire class where different types of books are located. Be sure they understand the difference between fiction and non-fiction and be sure they know how to find items that are arranged in alphabetical order. The worksheets on the pages in this section will help you with many of those skills.

Also be sure to read to your students some of the books mentioned on this page. On April 27, for example, you may want to read to your students many of the *Madeline* books. Then take them to the library and help them to discover how to find Bemelmans' books in the library.

Math in the Library

In addition to the math activities on pages 227-228, here's a fun activity with estimating, counting and multiplying:

- Ask your students to estimate the number of books on one shelf in the library. First each student could guess how many books are on it and write that number down. Then ask someone to count them to get the actual number. Find out who had the closest guess.

- If your students are able to understand very large numbers, ask them to next estimate how many books are in the entire library. Allow them to use calculators to multiply the number of books per shelf by the number of shelves (either estimated or counted) in the library. Check students' estimates with the librarian to find out who's guess is the closest.

Lola's Library

Lola wants very much to get to the library in her town. But she's just moved in and can't remember how to get there. Draw a path through the maze to help Lola find her library.

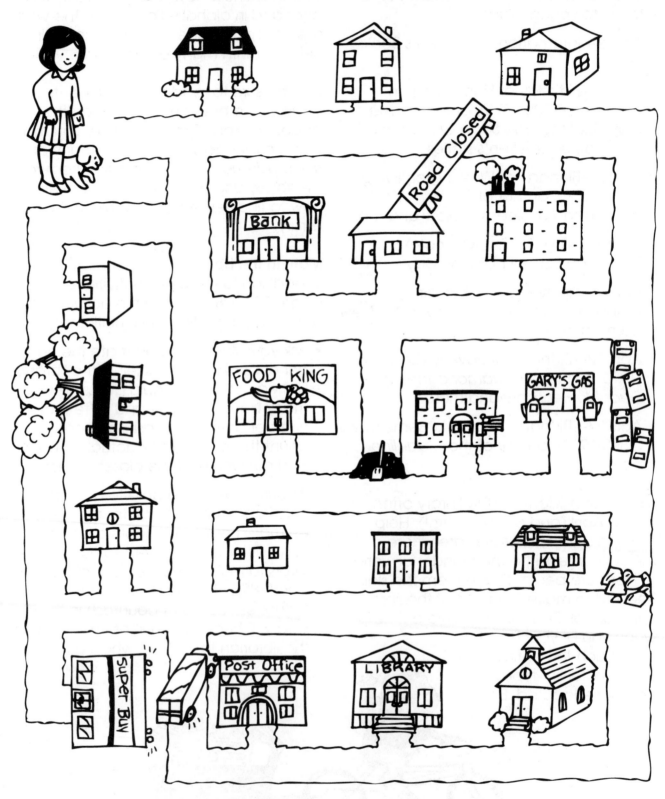

On the back of this page, draw a picture of how Lola's library might look on the inside.

TLC10408 Copyright © Teaching & Learning Company, Carthage, IL 62321-0010

Name _____

Was It Real?

Some stories tell about facts that really happened. Some stories tell only about make-believe events. Books that are true are called non-fiction. Books that are make-believe are called fiction.

Read the name of each book below. Write N on the blank if it is non-fiction, or true. Write F in the blank if it is fiction, or make-believe.

1. A dictionary _____

2. *Winnie-the-Pooh* _____

3. A book about the history of the United States _____

4. A book about Bugs Bunny _____

5. *Cinderella* _____

6. A book about weather _____

7. A book that tells how to fix a car _____

8. A book about a talking dog _____

9. A book about a beanstalk that you can climb a mile high _____

10. A book of sports records _____

At your library, find the titles of three non-fiction books.

_____

_____

Now write the titles of two fiction books.

_____

_____

Name _____

Authors' Order

In most libraries, fiction books are put on the shelf in ABC order by the author's last name.
Here is how one set of library books might look:

Insects That Talk
by C. Bee

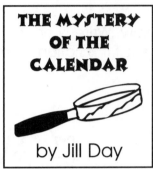

THE MYSTERY OF THE CALENDAR
by Jill Day

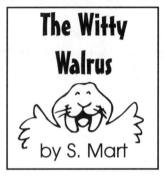

The Witty Walrus
by S. Mart

Down Here
by Cee Up

Now write these names and titles on the ends of the books at the bottom of the page.
Write them in ABC order by the author's last name.
You may write only the last name of the author on each book.

1. *I'm Glad* by Bea Happy

2. *Talking Animals* by Pete Pets

3. *Mary Smith* by Jane Doe

4. *Crazy Pairs* by A. Match

5. *Numbers* by Juan Two

6. *Clean Up* by Ima Dirty

7. *Fairy Tales* by A. Princess

8. *The Magical Town* by F. Hanks

9. *Trust Me* by I.M. Honest

10. *Missing Coins* by Penny Dime

1	2	3	4	5	6	7	8	9	10

Name _____

Writing a thank-you note

Dear Librarian

Are you glad that your librarian is at school to keep your library open and help you check out good books? Wouldn't it be nice if you could tell him or her how much you appreciate him or her? A note of thanks or appreciation is a good way to do that. Complete the letter below. Be sure to use complete sentences, correct spelling and neat handwriting.

Heading _____

_____

_____

Greeting

Dear _____,

_____

_____

_____

_____

Body

_____

_____

_____

_____

Closing _____

_____

Name _____

Program Notes

The Fisher Elementary School library is holding a special program for National Library Week. This is the sign on the library door. You can see that the sentences need to have a (.) or a (?) at the end. Add a (.) at the end of the telling sentences. Add a (?) at the end of the asking sentences.

Library Program

1. The library will be open from 9 o'clock to 6 o'clock

2. Have your read any good books lately

3. Come and tell the librarian about them

4. Do you know where to find non-fiction books

5. Learn about where to find special books

6. Will your parents be able to come to our program

7. The library is here for you to use

8. Please enjoy your school library

9. Please keep the library clean

10. Did you tell the librarian you are glad she's here for you

Name _____

Adding with regrouping
Check It Out!

Ten sets of twins checked out a bunch of books at the Twin City Library. Add the number of books checked out by each pair of children. Write your answers in the blanks.

1. Ann checked out 13 books.
   Jan checked out 17.
   Total: _____

2. Amy checked out 25 magazines.
   Ramie checked out 16 magazines.
   Total: _____

3. Gary checked out 9 CDs.
   Mary checked out 18 CDs.
   Total: _____

4. Matt checked out 14 books.
   Pat checked out 17 books.
   Total: _____

5. During all of April, Ruby checked
   out 36 books. Rose borrowed 46.
   Total: _____

6. In April, Clyde borrowed 54 books.
   Claude borrowed 48 books.
   Total: _____

7. Sam checked out 52 magazines.
   Pam checked out 49.
   Total: _____

8. Stan borrowed 38 books.
   Fran checked out 33.
   Total: _____

9. Molly checked out 67 books during April.
   Polly checked out 76 books.
   Total: _____

10. Al checked out 59 books during April.
    Sal borrowed 44.
    Total: _____

Name _____

That's Not So Fine!

Larry Latebird has a hard time remembering when his library books are due. Everytime a book is late, he owes his library 3¢. Look at the calendar page. Read about Larry's late books. After each item, write the amount of the fine that Larry should pay.

April

1	2	3	4	5	6	7
8	9	10	11	12	13	14
15	16	17	18	19	20	21
22	23	24	25	26	27	28
29	30					

1. One book was due April 1. Larry returned it on April 5. He owes _____.

2. Another book was due April 4. He returned it on April 14. He owes _____.

3. Larry's magazine was due April 15. He returned it on April 27. Larry owes _____.

4. Larry had two books due on April 20. He returned both of them on April 29. Altogether, Larry owes _____ for both books.

5. A CD was due on April 13. Larry returned it on April 29. He owes _____.

6. Larry should have returned 2 magazines on April 11. But he turned them in 11 days late. On what date did Larry return them? _____

7. Larry's last 4 books were due on April 25. He returned them on April 30. He owes _____ in all for the 4 books.

Name _____

Be Kind to Animals Week

second week of April

Look at the pictures. Read the question. Write an answer to the question on the line.

What will Jim do?

_____

How will Mia help the new kittens?

_____

Name _____

Look at the pictures. Read the question. Write an answer to the question on the line.

What will Jose feed his horse?

_____

Will Sue call the vet?

_____

Name _____

Animal Letters

Say the name of each animal. Write the first and last letter of its name in the blanks.

___ ro ___

___ a ___

___ oa ___

___ io ___

___ i ___

___ o ___

___ kun ___

___ abbi ___

___ ea ___

Name ______________________________

Capital letters, ABC order

Capital Animals

These animals all have names. Their names are proper nouns, and proper nouns always begin with capital letters. Write these names in the blanks below, and spell each name with a capital letter.

snoopy mickey mouse garfield bugs bunny miss piggy tweety bird

On the back, write the names of two more famous animals. Use capital letters.

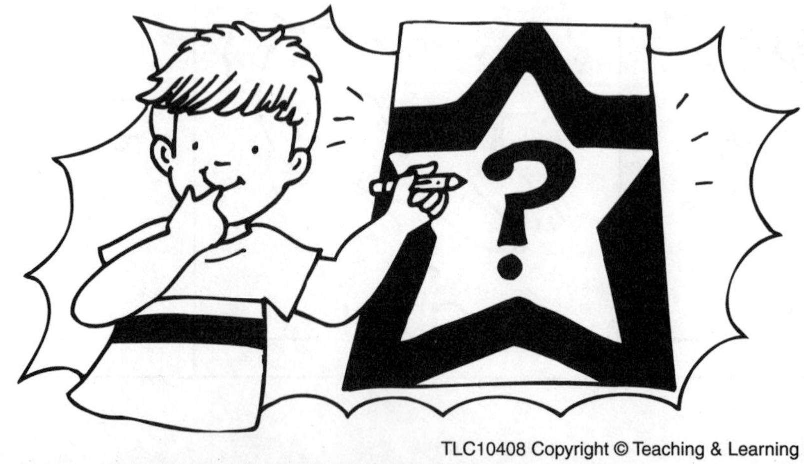

Adjectives

What Kind of Cat?

You may remember that adjectives are words that describe objects. During Be Kind to Animals Week, you may be thinking about the animals that you care about.
If you were to pick up a cat and hold it in your arms, how could you describe it?
Here are some adjectives you might use:

soft   warm   cuddly   furry   sleepy   playful

Can you think of another word to describe a cat? Write it here: _____

Read the words in each line below. Circle the ones that are adjectives. Then add one more describing word of your own on the blank at the end.

1. hamster   quick   hungry   run   eat   tiny   _____

2. sheep   lazy   graze   woolly   follow   soft   _____

3. duck   quack   wet   swim   feathered   brown   _____

4. turtle   tough   quiet   slippery   water   food   _____

5. parakeet   small   noisy   friendly   beak   blue   _____

6. poodle   funny   haircut   proud   white   dog   _____

7. snail   shell   sticky   eyes   slimy   slow   _____

8. cheetah   quick   race   spotted   wild   win   _____

9. alligator   hide   dangerous   green   prickly   mouth   _____

10. skunk   smelly   striped   nose   scent   black   _____

Name _____

Counting, addition

Pet Shop

Can you help count the animals at the pet shop? First count the number of animals in each pen or cage. Write the number under the cage. Then add the numbers together in each row. Write that number in the box at the end of the row.

Row 1

_____   _____   _____

Row 2

_____   _____   _____

Row 3

_____   _____   _____

Name _____

Pet Shop Prices

A certain shop sells pets in an unusual way. The animals are priced according to the spelling of the animal name. First look at the chart and see that A = $1, B = $2 on through Z = $26. Then find the price for the animals listed by adding the correct numbers together.

Example: CAT = 3 + 1 + 20 = $24   A cat sells for $24.

Before you find the prices, first try to make some predictions.
Which animal do you think will cost the most? Circle it.
Which do you think will cost the least? Underline it.

A	= $1
B	= $2
C	= $3
D	= $4
E	= $5
F	= $6
G	= $7
H	= $8
I	= $9
J	= $10
K	= $11
L	= $12
M	= $13
N	= $14
O	= $15
P	= $16
Q	= $17
R	= $18
S	= $19
T	= $20
U	= $21
V	= $22
W	= $23
X	= $24
Y	= $25
Z	= $26

1. DOG _____

2. LAMB _____

3. PIG _____

4. PARROT _____

5. TURKEY _____

6. MOUSE _____

7. SNAKE _____

8. CRAB _____

Were your predictions correct?

Name _____

Completeing a bar graph
Life Spans

Do you know how long your pet is expected to live? This chart shows the average life span of some common animals. Read it carefully.

Now complete the bar graph below. Make a bar for each kind of animal to show how long it is expected to live.

Animal	Average Life Span
Cats	12 years
Dogs	12 years
Guinea Pigs	4 years
Hamsters	2 years
Horses	20 years
Rabbits	5 years
Slider Turtles	15 years

Average Life Span of Some Common Animals

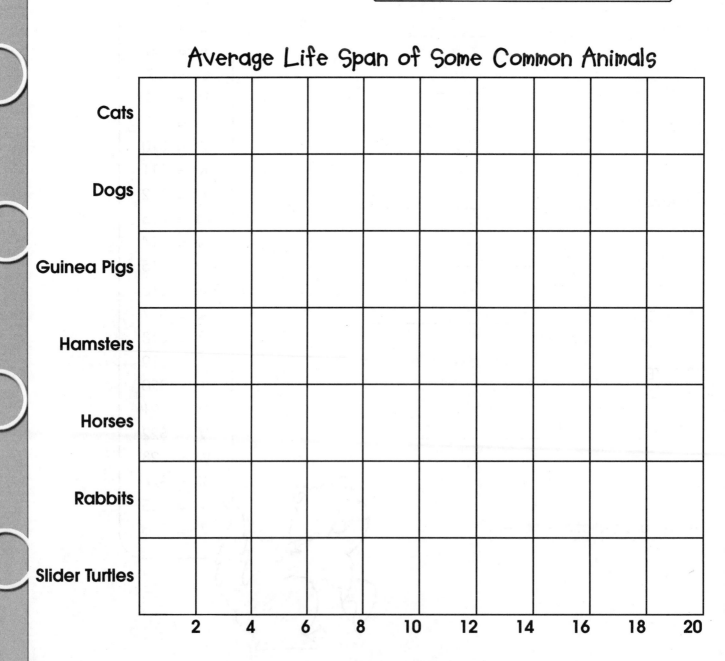

Easter

Use this pattern for take-home Easter cards. Instruct students to color the card and fill in the blanks. You may also want them to glue cotton on the bunny on the front.

signed

From
some
"bunny"
who loves you!

Special Message

Fold here first

Fold here second

To: _____

Hoppy Easter

Shape Book Pattern

EASTER GREETINGS

Name _____

Easter Egg Hunt

Circle the two Easter eggs that match. Then color all of the eggs.

A   B   C

D   E   F

G   H   I

Name _____

Egg Baskets

Color the eggs at the bottom of the page. Then cut them out and glue each one in the right basket. Be sure to get four eggs in each basket.

Multiples of 5

Odd numbers

Numbers larger than 30

10   5   30   20   42   36

54   31   13   27   19   7

Awards & Name Tags

This award is for

_____

in recognition of excellent work during

National Poetry Month

I'm helping
to keep

America

beautiful!

name

Dear

May you have
a wonderful
Easter
holiday!
Enjoy your
vacation, and
don't eat too
many
chocolate
eggs!

From your teacher,

_____

Bookmarks

Summer

Get ready for a magnificent May and a stupendous summer! Here is a fresh assortment of bulletin boards, teacher helps and curriculum reproducible pages to see you through many of the special days in May and summer.

We've chosen several special themes: Bicycle Safety Month, Mother Goose Day, Cinco de Mayo, Mother's Day, patriotic holidays, Little League Baseball Week, Father's Day and summer vacation. For some of these themes you will find bulletin boards, a poem and resource lists. For all of the units you will have appealing reproducibles that cover important primary skills. Most skill sheets are for math or language, but we've also included some pages for science, social studies and general thinking skills.

Pick the themes you are most interested in and select activities and worksheets that are on an appropriate level for your students. You will be able to use many ideas in each unit even though some individual pages may be too difficult or too simple for your particular class.

First your students will learn about bicycle safety. On pages 245-255 you'll find a bulletin board idea. There is a teacher page with safety rules and a student quiz. There are also student reproducibles featuring a crossword puzzle, analogies, a math code and more.

For Mother Goose Day and Cinco de Mayo, we've covered more important language, math and thinking skills. You won't want to miss the page of look-alike Mother Geese and the lists of Spanish number and color words.

Mother's Day and Father's Day both receive equal attention with reproducibles for unique cards. Included are skill pages that provide practice with dictionary skills, possessives, animal names, fractions, coin values and more. Your students are bound to enjoy reading together the Father's Day choral reading on page 290.

Memorial Day, Flag Day and Independence Day are all addressed on pages 271-279. Especially helpful are the tips for proper care of the flag and party foods listed on the teacher page. The resource list on page 279 will provide you with plenty of helpful books on the American flag, Pledge and patriotic songs and holidays.

Little League Baseball Week and summer vacation are the final topics. Here again, you'll find plenty of skill practice to keep your students learning all year long!

Don't forget all the great bonus clip art on the CD. It promises to make for a truly magnificent May and a stupendous summer in your classroom!

Bicycle Safety Month

May is Bicycle Safety Month. The bulletin board on pages 246-248 will help introduce your students to this important topic. Children may already know some safety rules that can be included on the display. Brainstorm together to make a list on the chalkboard. Here are some:

- Before you get on your bike, put on a helmet. Also wear gloves, knee pads and elbow pads if possible.

- Be sure your bike is in good condition before you ride. Check the brakes and tires.

- Never ride out into a street without stopping first.

- Obey stop signs.

- Check behind you before you turn, swerve or change lanes.

- Keep following the rules, even when you are riding behind another bicyclist.

- If riding a bike at night:

    - Always use a headlight.

    - Be sure your bike has front and rear reflectors pedal flectors and side rim or wheel reflectors.

    - Wear reflective clothing.

    - Avoid riding on dark, narrow roadways.

    - Remember that young children should not ride at night.

Remember to review bicycle safety rules several times during the month. When you think your students have a good understanding of bike safety, ask them to take the safety quiz on page 249.

You'll find several language and math activities on pages 250-254. A resource list is given on page 255. You'll find some comprehensive information books as well as a variety of picture books filled with fun stories about fictional bikes and bikers. Don't let May run out before your students hear *Curious George Rides a Bike* or *Duck on a Bike*.

Bicycle Safety Month

Draw a curvy road on the background of your bulletin board. Use colored chalk or charcoal. Ask students to cut out several bikes and characters using the patterns on pages 247-248. Then add "callouts" so that each cyclist is speaking a safety rule. Use rules listed by your students, or ones that appear on page 245.

248

Name _____

Bike Quiz

Are you a safe bicyclist? Take this quiz and find out.
Circle the best answer to each question.

1. When you ride a bike a night, what do you need?

   A. dark colored clothes   B. your walkman   C. clothes that reflect light

2. Every time you ride your bike, you should obey

   A. all traffic rules   B. some traffic rules   C. no traffic rules

3. You need to stop when you come to a red light or stop sign

   A. when there are cars behind you   B. only if you see traffic ahead of you

   C. every single time

4. You need to wear a helmet because

   A. it looks cool   B. it protects you   C. it was a birthday present

5. When you are riding in the street with other big vehicles, you should always stay on the _____ side of the road.

   A. left   B. right   C. center

6. Be sure your bike is ready to ride with a:

   A. rear-view mirror   B. a white light for night   C. both of these

7. Before you turn or change lanes, you should

   A. check behind you   B. ask permission from other riders   C. stop

8. In addition to a helmet, it is a good idea to wear

   A. a life jacket   B. a hat   C. knee and elbow pads

9. Before riding on a road, be sure you know how to use your

   A. brakes   B. basket   C. coat

10. When you are riding behind another bicyclist, you should

   A. follow everything he does   B. follow all the safety rules   C. honk your horn

Draw a picture on the back of you and your dream bike.

Name _____

Crossword puzzle
Barb's Bicycle

Barb and *bicycle* are words that begin with B.
Use the picture clues to fill in the crossword with some other words that begin with B.

Clues

Across

1

3

4

5

Down

1

2

3

4

Name _____

Who Likes Bikes?

Do you know who likes bikes? Two boys named Mike and Ike like bikes because their names rhyme! Read the sentences below. Find a name in the word bank that rhymes with the word in bold type. Write a rhyming person's name in each blank.

1. _____ wants to ride a **train**.

2. _____ hopes to drive a big **truck**.

3. _____ rides in the **trailer**.

4. _____ will take a **ship**.

5. _____ loves to ride in the **car**.

6. _____ always takes her **van**.

7. _____ will ride the **bus**.

Word Bank

Chip
Taylor
Gus
Dar
Jan
Shane
Buck

Name _____

Let's Think!

An analogy lets you compare sets that are related in the same way.
You know that a wheel is part of a bike. And you know that a roof is part of a house.
So you could say wheel is to bike as roof is to house.
You can use : as a symbol for the words *is to* and = as a symbol for *as*, so . . .
wheel : bike = roof : house

Think about what the first two words have in common.
Then circle the word that makes sense in the analogy.

1. flower : tulip = fruit : _____

2. sock : foot = glove : _____

3. see : eyes = hear : _____

4. horse : pony = bear : _____

5. swim : water = ski : _____

6. listen : music = read : _____

7. skin : human = feathers : _____

8. cow : farm = duck : _____

Name _____

Bicycle Shop

Look at all the bikes in Barb's Bicycle Shop! Study the picture carefully.
Then answer the questions at the bottom of the page.

1. How many two-wheelers do you see? _____ Circle the bicycles.

2. Find the two-wheeler with the most spokes. How many spokes are there on both

   wheels? _____

3. A unicycle has just one wheel. How many do you see? _____ Color the unicycles.

4. A tricycle has three wheels. How many tricycles do you see? _____ Draw an X
   on the tricycles.

5. Now count all the wheels in the shop–the wheels from unicycles, bicycles and tricy-

   cles all together. How many wheels did you count? _____

Name _____

Sums to 20, solving a code

Riding Riddle

Why can't a bicycle stand up by itself? To find out the answer to this riddle, solve the math problems below. Use the code box to find a letter that matches each answer. Then write the letters in the blanks at the bottom of the page. The first one is done for you.

1. 9 + 9 = __18__

2. 12 + 8 = _____

3. 6 + 7 = _____

4. 3 + 7 = _____

5. 14 + 5 = _____

6. 6 + 5 = _____

7. 9 + 11 = _____

8. 7 + 8 = _____

9. 5 + 7 = _____

10. 9 + 6 = _____

11. 4 + 7 = _____

12. 6 + 6 = _____

13. 8 + 9 = _____

14. 12 + 5 = _____

15. 3 + 9 = _____

16. 4 + 11 = _____

17. 7 + 7 = _____

18. 4 + 16 = _____

19. 8 + 8 = _____

Code
10 = A
11 = S
12 = T
13 = C
14 = R
15 = I
16 = D
17 = O
18 = B
19 = U
20 = E

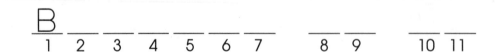

B __ __ __ __ __ __ __   __ __   __ __
1 2 3 4 5 6 7   8 9   10 11

__ __ __   __ __ __ __ __!
12 13 14   15 16 17 18 19

Resources

Information Books

Bicycle Book by Gail Gibbons. Holiday House, Inc., 1995.
This includes a brief history of bicycles, as well as information on different kinds of bikes, how they work and the different ways they are used. This resource also includes safety tips for bike riders and guidelines for bike maintenance.

Bicycle Safety by Rudolf Steiner. The Child's World, Inc., 1996.

Bicycling by Bill Gutman. Capstone Press, 1995.

Picture Books

The Bear's Bicycle by Emilie Warren McLeod. Little, Brown & Company, 1997.

Bicycle Man by Allen Say. Houghton Mifflin Company, 1989.

Curious George Rides a Bike by H.A. Rey. Houghton Mifflin Co., 1973.

Duck on a Bike by David Shannon. Scholastic, Inc., 2002

Henry and Beezus by Beverly Cleary. HarperCollins Children's Books, 1990.

Julian's Glorious Summer by Ann Cameron. Random House, Inc., 1987.

Let's Go Froggy! by Jonathan London. The Penguin Group, 1996.

Marvin Redpost: Super Fast, Out of Control! by Louis Sachar. Random House, Inc., 2000.

My Rows and Piles of Coins by Tololwa M. Mollel and Earl Lewis. Houghton Mifflin Co., 1999.

Poppleton in Spring by Cynthia Rylant. Scholastic, Inc., 1998.

The Red Racer by Audrey Wood. Simon & Schuster, Reprint, 1999.

Shape Book Pattern

Teacher: Mother Goose Day is observed annually on May 1.
Use this shape book for your students to record their favorite nursery rhymes.

Name _____

Look-Alikes

These may all look like the same Mother Goose, but there are really only two that are exactly the same. Can you find them? Circle the two geese that match. Then color all of them.

A.

B.

C.

D.

E.

Name _____

Hey, Diddle, Diddle!

Do you know the nursery rhyme "Hey, Diddle, Diddle"?
Think about the events that happen in it. Look at the pictures below.
Number them from 1 to 4, in the same order that they happen in the nursery rhyme.

Now put these sentences in order, too.

_____ The cow jumped over the moon.

_____ The dish ran away with the spoon.

_____ The cat and the fiddle.

_____ The little dog laughed to see such a sport.

Name _____

Ready for Action

Do you remember the actions from many nursery rhymes? Draw a line to connect each beginning to the correct ending of the sentence. You will make 12 sentences that tell what action takes place in several nursery rhymes.

1. Little Jack Horner	A. followed her to school one day.
2. The cat	B. ran up the clock.
3. The cow	C. lived in a shoe.
4. Little-Bo-Peep	D. ate no fat.
5. Jack Sprat	E. walked up a hill.
6. Mary's little lamb	F. jumped over the moon.
7. Simple Simon	G. sat on a wall, but then he had a great fall.
8. Humpty Dumpty	H. played the fiddle.
9. Jack and Jill	I. ran all the way home.
10. A woman with many children	J. sat in a corner.
11. The mouse	K. met a pie man.
12. This little piggy	L. lost her sheep.

Now look back over the words in the right-hand column. Circle the action verb in each line. Copy one complete sentence from your matching above. Write it on the back of this page. Draw a picture that goes with your sentence.

Name _____

Solving word problems, addition, subtraction, multiplication
Mother Goose Math

Read each word problem. Write a math sentence to help you answer the question. Then add, subtract or multiply to find the answer. Write your answer in the second blank.

1. The old woman in the shoe had so many children, she didn't know what to do! She counted 6 children on the first floor, 8 on the second floor and 5 more on the top floor. How many children did she have in all? _____ Answer: _____

2. Three little kittens lost all of their mittens. How many mittens did they have? _____ Answer: _____

3. In "Rub-a-Dub-Dub," there were 3 men in a tub. How many men would there be in 7 tubs? _____ Answer: _____

4. If you counted the feet on all 5 pigs in "This Little Pig Went to Market," how many feet would there be? _____ Answer: _____

5. Jack Sprat could eat no fat, so he often lost weight. In May he lost 4 pounds, in June he lost 7 pounds and in July he lost 3 pounds. How many pounds altogether did he lose in those three months? _____ Answer: _____

6. Jack and Jill were running down the hill with a 12-gallon pail of water. When they fell down the hill, they spilled 9 gallons of the water. How many gallons were left in the pail? _____ Answer: _____

7. Little Jack Horner wanted to help his mother make plum pie. He washed 17 plums for her to use. Mrs. Horner decided that there were too many plums for one pie, so she didn't use 6 of them. How many plums did she use for Jack's pie? _____ Answer: _____

8. The big clock is 63 inches tall. The mouse ran up the clock and back down the clock. How many inches did he travel in all? _____ Answer: _____

9. After Humpty Dumpty's fall, all the kings' men worked hard to put him back together. 9 men worked for 4 hours each. How many hours were spent in all on Humpty? _____ Answer: _____

10. Simple Simon met a pie man going to the fair. But he didn't have much money with him. The smallest pie cost 89¢. Simon gave the pie man one dollar. How much change should Simon receive? _____ Answer: _____

Name _____

Cinco de Mayo

Cinco de Mayo is a Mexican holiday filled with fun, food, flowers and festivals.
Cinco means "five" in Spanish. Read the Spanish names for other numbers:

1 one uno	6 six seis
2 two dos	7 seven siete
3 three tres	8 eight ocho
4 four cuatro	9 nine nueve
5 five cinco	10 ten diez

Count the number of items in each box.
Write the Spanish word for the correct number in the blank.

Multiples of 5
Hidden Picture

Here's a fun Cinco de Mayo activity. Look at the numbered spaces below. If a space shows a number that is a multiple of 5 (5, 10, 15, 20, etc.), color it with a crayon or colored pencil. If the space does not show a multiple of 5, leave it blank.

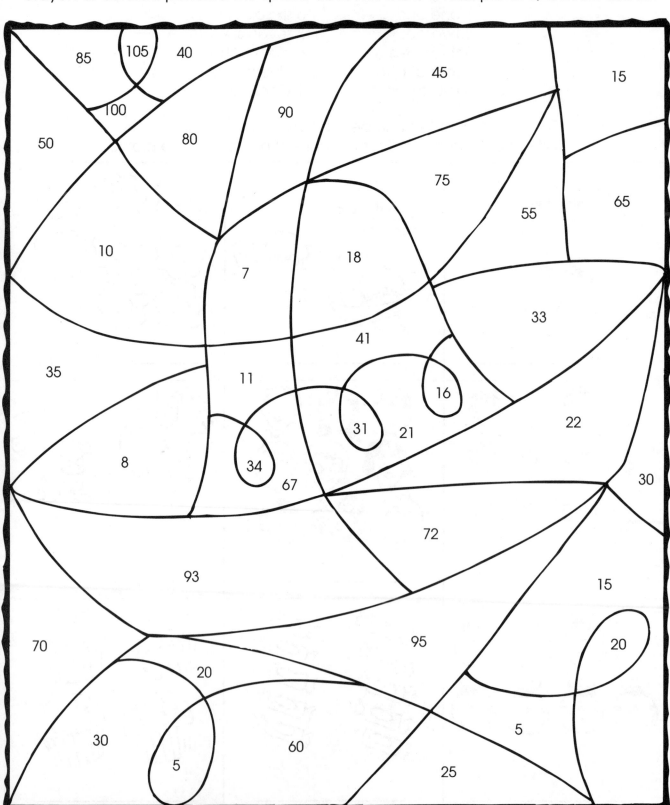

Name _____

Color words
Scrambled Colors

Celebrate Cinco de Mayo by learning Spanish words for colors. Seven of these words are listed here. Unscramble the letters following each Spanish word to spell the English word for the same color. Then color the border by coloring the numbered spaces with the color that matches each number.

1. rojo = _____ (erd)

2. azul = _____ (lebu)

3. verde = _____ (nereg)

4. blanco = _____ (hewit)

5. amarillo = _____ (lolewy)

6. purpureo = _____ (rulppe)

7. moreno = _____ (wrobn)

Mother's Day

Help your students show their love and appreciation for their mothers in some fun new ways. On pages 265 and 266, you'll find a Mother's Day card filled with easy recipes. Plan ahead to make one, two or all three of these recipes in class with your students before Mother's Day. Then the students will already know how tasty (and how easy) these recipes are when they present the cards to their moms. Photocopy pages 265-266 following the directions below. Give students time to color their Mother's Day cards before taking the cards home.

Instructions for Photocopying
Duplicate page B on the back of page A, like this:

front   back

Encourage your students to complete Mother's Day "coupons" to tuck inside their cards. Coupons should be good for simple deeds such as setting the table, washing dishes, hugs or other non-monetary items. Here are two sample coupons you may want to use:

You will also want to use the language and math reproducibles on pages 267-270. Your students can practice using possessives, learn about animal names, solve fun puzzles with fractions and more.

Mother's Day Card

Peachy Cake-Cobbler

Mom: You should melt the margarine in the microwave and place the pan in and out of the oven. Your child can do the rest! This can bake at the same time as the macaroni recipe.

1 29-oz. can sliced peaches
1 18-oz. box yellow or white cake mix
1/2 cup melted margarine
1/2 cup chopped walnuts or pecans

Pour peaches with juice into a 9" x 13" pan. Sprinkle dry cake mix evenly over peaches. Drizzle melted better over top. Sprinkle nuts on. Bake at 350°F for 50-60 minutes.

Happy Mother's Day!

I hope this day is special for you.
There's something nice I'd like to do.
I'll help you cook and bake, you see.
Just look inside for a recipe!

Mother's Day Card

Red Hot Salad

Mom: You should handle the boiling water; your child can stir the candy for several minutes until it dissolves.

1 3-oz. package of strawberry Jello®
3 teaspoons red hot cinnamon candies
1 cup boiling water
1 cup applesauce

Dissolve Jello® in $1/2$ cup of boiling water. Dissolve the candies in the other $1/2$ cup of boiling water. Combine the two solutions and add the applesause. Pour into a pretty dish and refrigerate until the salad is firm.

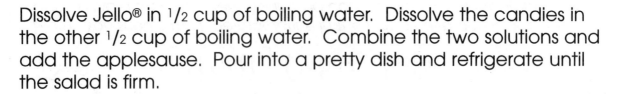

Easy-Cheesey Macaroni

Mom: You should handle the pan in and out of the oven.

Mix this one the day before you plan to eat it.

2 cups dry macaroni
2 cans cream of mushroom soup
3 cups milk
6 oz. dried beef or other meat
8 oz. cubed sharp cheese

Mix all ingredients together in a large bowl. Cover and store overnight in the refrigerator. Stir before pouring into a 9" x 13" pan. Bake uncovered for one hour at 350°F.

Dictionary skills
May Flowers

May Day and Mother's Day mean lots of beautiful flowers! Suppose that you are trying to learn about all different kinds of flowers. Shown below is a list of 20 kinds of flowers. If you were to look up each word in a dictionary, would you find it near the beginning, in the middle or near the end?

Write B for beginning, M for middle or E for end.

_____ 1. aster   _____ 11. pansy

_____ 2. marigold   _____ 12. bluebell

_____ 3. zinnia   _____ 13. violet

_____ 4. forget-me-not   _____ 14. orchid

_____ 5. lily   _____ 15. dahlia

_____ 6. rose   _____ 16. snapdragon

_____ 7. carnation   _____ 17. narcissus

_____ 8. wisteria   _____ 18. tulip

_____ 9. lilac   _____ 19. azalea

_____ 10. daffodil   _____ 20. sunflower

Draw a picture of your favorite flower on the back of this page.

Name _____

Mother's Work

Mothers are very busy both in and out of the home. Here are the names and pictures of six different mothers, along with six items they might use for their jobs. First, draw a line from each mother to show what belongs to her.

Sally   Nan   Jill   Pam   Deb   Mary

Now write a sentence to answer each question below.
Remember to use an apostrophe (') and an **s** after the name of the owner.

Example: Whose beach towel is this? This is Clara's beach towel.

1. Whose brush is that?

_____

2. Who owns the slippers?

_____

3. To whom does the rolling pin belong?

_____

4. Whose X ray is that?

_____

5. Who owns the rope?

_____

Science—animal names

Mothers on Parade

Look at the animal parade! Many animal mothers decided to have a Mother's Day parade, but they are not standing in the right order. Look at the picture. Then follow the directions below to help get the animal mothers in the correct places.

1. The calf's mother wanted to go first in the parade. Find her and put a 1 on her.

2. The fawn's mother wanted to go second. Put a 2 on her.

3. Put a 3 on the lamb's mother.

4. Put a 4 on the bunny's mother.

5. Put a 5 on the kid's mother.

6. Put a 6 on the colt's mother.

7. Put a 7 on the chick's mother.

8. Put a 8 on the puppy's mother.

9. The last mother was the one that belonged to the kitten. Put an 9 on the kitten's mother.

Mother's Day Gifts

Read each gift. Join the letters and tell what Mother's Day gift is inside.
The first one has been done for you.

3/4 of cans
1/3 of dog
1/4 of yarn

1. c a n d y

1/4 of hand
1/2 of up
1/3 of gum
1/4 of slip

2. _ _ _ _ _

2/3 of rip
1/4 of nest
1/4 of grin

3. _ _ _ _ _

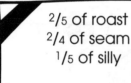

2/5 of roast
2/4 of seam
1/5 of silly

4. _ _ _ _ _ _

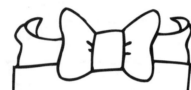

1/3 of day
2/5 of ready
1/4 of slam
1/5 of skunk

5. _ _ _ _ _

1/4 of mine
2/5 of usual
2/3 of ice

6. _ _ _ _ _

1/3 of dad
2/4 of into
2/4 of next
1/3 of red

7. _ _ _ _ _

1/2 of picnic
3/4 of turn
1/4 of easy

8. _ _ _ _ _ _ _

1/5 of leave
2/4 of oven
1/3 of ear

9. _ _ _ _

270

Patriotic Holidays

Stir up some national pride as you celebrate the patriotic holidays that fall during May, June and July! Memorial Day, Flag Day (June 14) and Independence Day (July 4) all provide opportunities to teach your students about America's history and their own national heritage. The special resources listed on page 279 will be invaluable during these summer holidays. Some of these books cover history, some contain illustrated versions of patriotic songs and some give information about specific holidays.

Notice the language and math activities on pages 274-278. These cover important skills and follow the patriotic theme as well. In case you're sending any letters to parents during these holidays, we've included a patriotic stationery form on page 273.

Some additional suggestions for Memorial Day, Flag Day and/or Independence Day:

- Practice saying the Pledge of Allegiance with your students. Be sure they know the meaning of all the words. Ask students to copy it for some good handwriting practice.

- On the Fourth of July, ask your students to sing "Happy Birthday" to America.

- Teach your students the words to songs such as "America the Beautiful" and "The Star-Spangled Banner." Write a few lines at a time on the chalkboard. Then erase one or two words at a time, and see if children can remember the missing words. Once they master the first verses, challenge them to learn the words to additional verses. Again, be sure students understand the words they are singing.

- Teach your students proper care and use of the American flag:

1. The flag should always be flown with respect. Fly it only in good weather. It can be flown every day, or just on all holidays and special occasions.

2. The flag should be flown only from sunrise to sunset. If it is displayed at night, it should be lit.

3. The flag should normally be flown at full staff. It is flown at half staff to mark the death of an official.

4. When handling the flag, never let it touch the ground.

5. When the American flag flies with other flags, it should be above them.

6. When hung flat against a wall, the stars should be to the audience's left.

7. Salute the flag when it passes in a parade, when it is being raised or lowered, when it is present at the playing of the national anthem or when it is present at the reciting of the Pledge of Allegiance.

8. Civilians should salute the flag by standing at attention and placing their right hand over their heart. Men should remove their hats and hold them over their left shoulder with their right hand.

- Teach this little patriotic poem, or work together with your students to write a new one:

  America, we salute you.
  How we love the red, white and blue!
  America, we'll do our best
  To be sure this nation is blessed
  With kindness and sharing
  And genuine caring.
  America, we salute you!

Ask: What is meant by the red white and blue? (the American flag)

How can we be sure this nation "is blessed with kindness and sharing"? (by each of us being kind and sharing with one another)

What does *genuine* mean? (real, honest, sincere)

Finally, here are some red, white and blue recipes for your own patriotic party. Enjoy!

Red, White and Blue Sandwiches

Begin with a loaf of white sandwich bread. Trim the edges, if you like, to remove the crusts. For each sandwich, use three pieces of bread. Top the first slice of bread with blueberry jam or grape jelly. Add a slice of bread on top. Spread that slice of bread with strawberry or raspberry jam. Add a final slice on top. Cut the sandwich diagonally twice, to form four small triangles.

Red, White and Blue Parfaits

Begin with parfait glasses or clear disposable cups. Spoon vanilla yogurt into the bottom of each cup. Top with fresh blueberries. Layer more yogurt on top of the blueberries. Add a layer of fresh red raspberries, strawberries or strawberry jam. Top with a spoonful of yogurt. Sprinkle with chopped nuts, granola or Grape-Nuts® cereal.

Flag Cake

Bake any cake mix according to package directions in a 9" x 13" pan. When cool, frost with white frosting. Add blueberries in the top left corner (for stars) and rows of sliced ripe strawberries or fresh red raspberries (for stripes).

272

Name _____

Star Search

We know there are 50 stars on the American flag to represent each of our 50 states. Can you color 50 stars on this page? You may use any colors you like.

Name _____

Teacher: For young students, you may wish to do this orally. Write the possible categories on the chalkboard, and ask students which one fits with each group as you read the lists. Together, think of more items to add to each list.

Classification
Get a Group!

Read each list. All the things belong to a group, or category.
Add one more item to each list. Then write each group's classification.
Use the word box to help you. The first list has been done for you.

Presidents	parts of a flag	U.S. states
songs	sounds	American symbols

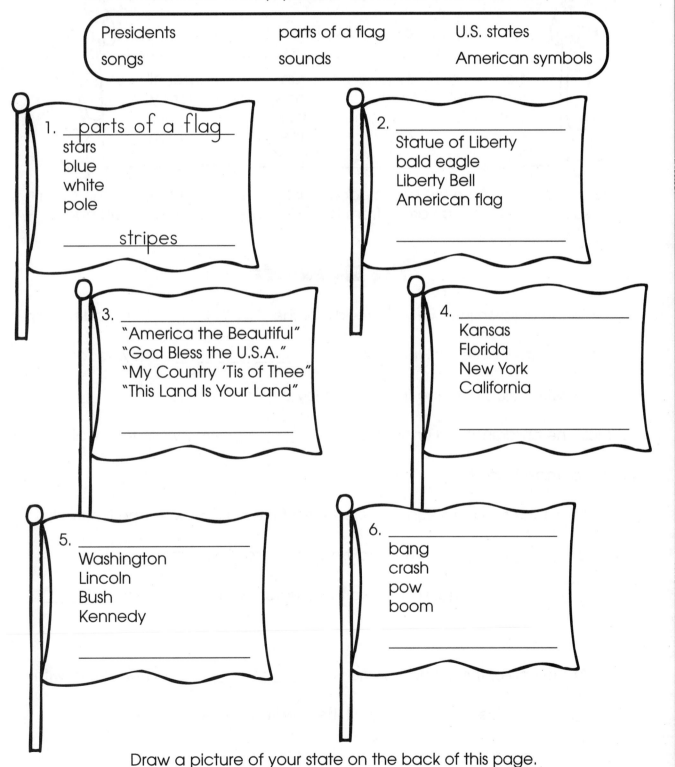

1. __parts of a flag__
stars
blue
white
pole

_____stripes_____

2. _____
Statue of Liberty
bald eagle
Liberty Bell
American flag
_____

3. _____
"America the Beautiful"
"God Bless the U.S.A."
"My Country 'Tis of Thee"
"This Land Is Your Land"
_____

4. _____
Kansas
Florida
New York
California

5. _____
Washington
Lincoln
Bush
Kennedy
_____

6. _____
bang
crash
pow
boom
_____

Draw a picture of your state on the back of this page.

Name _____

Patriotic Parade

You may remember that an adjective describes something.
The words in bold are adjectives in these sentences:
We flew our flag on a **windy** day.
The President is very **busy**.

Windy describes the day. *Busy* describes the President.

Circle the adjectives in this box.

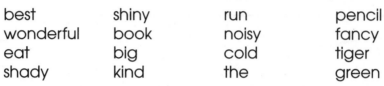

best	shiny	run	pencil
wonderful	book	noisy	fancy
eat	big	cold	tiger
shady	kind	the	green

Write an adjective from the box in each blank in this story. Underline the noun it describes, and draw an arrow from the adjective to the noun it tells about.

The Big Parade

All the children in town were ready for the _____ parade. They

had washed their bikes until the bikes were _____ . They decorated

the bikes with colors from the flag. Then they dressed in their _____

clothes. The children stood under the _____ tree while they waited

for the parade to start.

At last the parade began. The leaders of the parade were the fire trucks

with their _____ sirens. Next came the soldiers in their

_____ uniforms. Last came the children with their _____

bikes.

At the end of the parade, some very _____ ladies waited with

_____ ice cream cones! All the children agreed that was a

_____ surprise.

Name _____

Measure Up!

Cut out the ruler at the bottom of the page. Then measure each item to the nearest inch. Write the correct number in each blank.

1. How many inches long? _____

2. How many inches wide? _____

3. How many inches wide? _____

4. How many inches wide?

_____

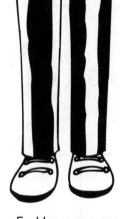

5. How many inches tall?

_____

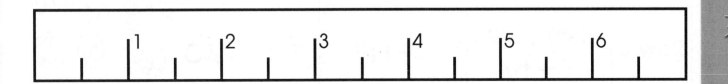

| | 1 | 2 | 3 | 4 | 5 | 6 |

Name _____

Fast 50

Mr. Five-O's class is studying the 50 states. He decided to ask each student to show a different way to write the number 50 for math class. Here are some of the answers he received. Some are right; some are not. Cross out each box that does not show 50 correctly.

	A	B	C	D
Row 1	fifty	5 + 10	60	(five dimes)
Row 2	50	卌 卌 卌 卌 卌 卌 卌 卌	20 + 30	fivety
Row 3	(2 quarters)	10 × 5	45 + 5	60 − 10
Row 4	20 + 40	five tens	(nine nickels)	卌 卌 卌 卌 卌 卌 卌 卌 卌 卌
Row 5	ten plus forty	25+15	70 − 20	(2 nickels and 4 dimes)

Resources

America: A Patriotic Primer by Lynne Cheney, Simon & Schuster Children's, 2002.

America Is. . . by Louise Borden. Margaret K. McElderry Books, 2002.

F Is for Flag by Wendy Cheyette Lewison. Penguin Putnam Books for Young Readers, 2002.

Flag Day by Kelly Bennet. Scholastic Library Publishing, 2003.

The 4th of July Story by Alice Dalgliesh, 2nd Aladdin Paperbacks Edition, June 1995.

Independence Day by Robin Nelson. Lerner Publishing Group, 2002.

I Pledge Allegiance by Bill Martin, et al. Candlewick Press, 2002.

I Pledge Allegiance (with cassette) by June Swanson. Live Oak Media, 1995.

Memorial Day by Jacqueline S. Cotton. Scholastic, 2002.

Memorial Day by Helen Frost. Capstone Press, 2000.

Red, White and Blue: The Story of the American Flag by John Herman. The Putnam Publishing Group, 1998.

Illustrated Children's Books Featuring Patriotic Songs

America the Beautiful by Katharine Lee Bates. Simon & Schuster Children's, 1993.

God, Bless America (book and CD) by Irving Berlin. HarperCollins Children's Books, 2002.

Star-Spangled Banner by Francis Scott Key, Random House Children's Books, 2002.

You're a Grand Old Flag by Marsha Qualey. Picture Window Books, 2003.

Poster Papers

We Love America! by Ann Richmond Fisher. Teaching & Learning Company, 2001.

Little League Baseball Week

Since 1959, Little League Baseball Week has been observed the week beginning with the second Monday in June. Don't let your Little Leaguers miss out on this great learning opportunity!

Begin by talking about what happens in a baseball game. Many of your students may already be on a T-ball team (which uses modified baseball rules) or Little League. Your players can help explain balls, strikes, outs, hits and runs in simple terms for the batting team. Explain the positions on the fielding team: pitcher; catcher; first, second and third basemen; shortstop and left, center and right fielders. Also tell students that the umpire stands behind home plate and decides if the pitch is a strike or a ball, if a runner is safe and so on. If possible, try to have your own classroom game of softball. To be sure that everyone gets a chance to play, you may want to use more than nine fielders, and allow more than three outs per inning. It's a great way to get some fresh air and exercise!

- To check your students' understanding of the game, and their own thinking skills, put this list of words on the board. Then ask them to sort the words into the proper categories.

- Here's another fun critical thinking activity. Ask your students to think about the uniforms baseball players wear. Each player has a different number. If there were just 9 players on the team, the uniforms could be numbered from 1 to 9, and only 1 of each digit would be required. However, if there were 10 players, two 1s would be required–first for the number 1, and secondly for the number 10. Continue in this same manner and ask your students to find these:

  - With 15 players, how many 5s are needed? (2: 5, 15) How many 1s? (8: 1, 10, 11, 12, 13, 14, 15)

  - With 20 players, how many 2s are needed? (3: 2, 12, 20) How many 1s? (12: 1,10, 11, 12, 13, 14, 15, 16, 17, 18, 19)

  - With 30 players, how many 3s are needed? (4) How many 1s? (13: all the numbers listed above, plus 21)

Word List

shortstop	safe	home plate
catcher	out	strike
first base	pitcher	center fielder
outfield	infield	ball

Categories

Baseball Positions
What an Umpire Says
Things on a Baseball Diamond

Name _____

Shapes
Get in Shape

Baseball is played on a diamond.

Look at this picture. Count the number of diamonds, triangles, squares and circles you see. Write the number next to the shape.

◇ _____   ☐ _____   △ _____   ◯ _____

Short vowel sounds

Shortstop Vowels

Say the word for each picture. The vowel is missing for each short vowel sound.
Write the correct vowel in the blank. The first one has been done for you.

s__cks	b__t	__mpire

p__tcher	p__pcorn	l__monade

r__unner	c__p	h__t d__g

Name _____

Batter Up!

Look at the picture of the baseball game. Think about what is going on.
Then write a story about it. It helps to write down your ideas first.

1. What will you name the characters in your story? _____

_____

2. How will the story begin? _____

_____

3. How will the story end? _____

_____

4. Now write your story. _____

_____

_____

_____

_____

_____

_____

_____

Name _____

Have a Ball!

Can you hit these words out of the park? Around the edge of each
baseball are letters that spell the name of something round. Start at a letter
and go around clockwise. Try starting with a different letter until you can
spell a common word. Write the word under the ball.

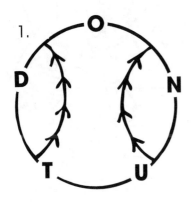

1.

_____

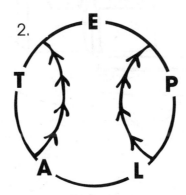

2.

_____

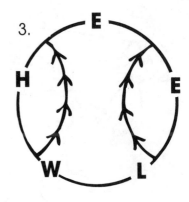

3.

_____

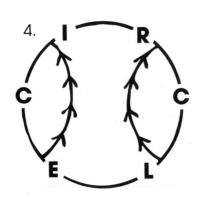

4.

_____

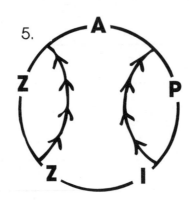

5.

_____

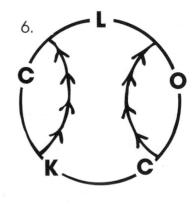

6.

_____

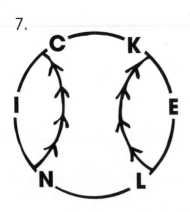

7.

_____

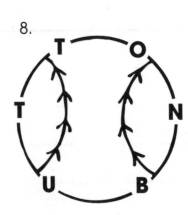

8.

_____

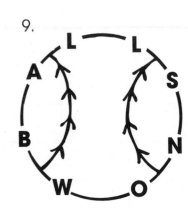

9.

_____

Name _____

Little League Logic

Can you find the answer to each of these questions? Read each one very carefully, and think about the possible answers. Write your final answer in each blank.

1. Rosa, Juan and Matt all play on the same baseball team. One is the pitcher, one is the catcher and one plays shortstop.
   A. The pitcher is a boy.
   B. Juan is the catcher.
   What position does Rosa play? _____

2. Rosa's baseball team wants to have a new team name. The 14 players have voted for one of these names: Eagles, Ponies or Panthers.
   A. The Eagles received six votes.
   B. The Ponies and Panthers both received the same number of votes.
   Which team name received the most votes? _____

3. Matt's aunt wants to go watch him play a game. She says to Matt, "If it's nice on Saturday and I can get off work, then I'll be at your game." Then she learns that Friday is her last day of work for the week. On Saturday, it is warm and sunny.
   Did Matt's aunt go to the game? _____

4. Juan's coach says, "If you missed any practices last week, or if you were late today, please raise your hand." Juan was at every practice last week, and he was on time today.
   Should he raise his hand? _____

5. Rosa is meeting her cousin, Marco, at the game. She's not seen Marco in three years, and after the game, she sees five kids who might be Marco. How will she know which boy is Marco? He sent her these clues:
   A. I never tie my shoelaces.
   B. I will wear sunglasses.
   C. I don't like shirts that button.
   Look at these five boys. Circle the one that is Marco.

Name _____

Logic, addition
Team Totals

Rosa's team played a game with the Tigers. The game lasted seven innings. The chart should show the number of runs that each team earned in each inning.

	1	2	3	4	5	6	7	Total
Eagles	2							
Tigers	2							

Both teams earned two runs in the first inning. Those numbers are shown in the chart. Now read these clues to find how many runs each team scored in the other innings.

A. The Eagles scored the same number of runs in the sixth inning as they did in the first.

B. The Tigers did not score in the fifth or seventh innings.

C. The Eagles did not score in the second or third innings.

D. Both teams scored 3 runs in the fourth inning.

E. The Tigers scored 1 more run in the sixth inning than the Eagles.

F. The Eagles scored 1 more run in the fifth inning than they did in the fourth inning.

G. In both the second and third innings, the Tigers scored 1 more run than the Eagles scored in those same innings.

H. The Eagles scored one run in the seventh inning.

After you have completed the chart to show how many runs each team earned in each inning, add the number of runs for each team and write their total score in the last boxes on the chart.

Which team won? _____

Father's Day

It's no puzzle to me...

You're the greatest!

Happy Father's Day!

from

_____

Can you solve this puzzle? First, cut out all these pieces. Then try to put them back together in the shape of a square and a rectangle.

Teacher: Here are two badges for Father's Day–one for students to cut
out and wear, and one for students to take home to their dads.

Father's Day Badges

June _____

20 _____

Happy Father's Day!

Dad

Fan of my Dad!

_____
name

_____
date

Name _____

A Father's Day Surprise

Look at each picture. Think about what is happening. Then finish the story by writing or drawing what you think will happen next. Use the last two boxes.

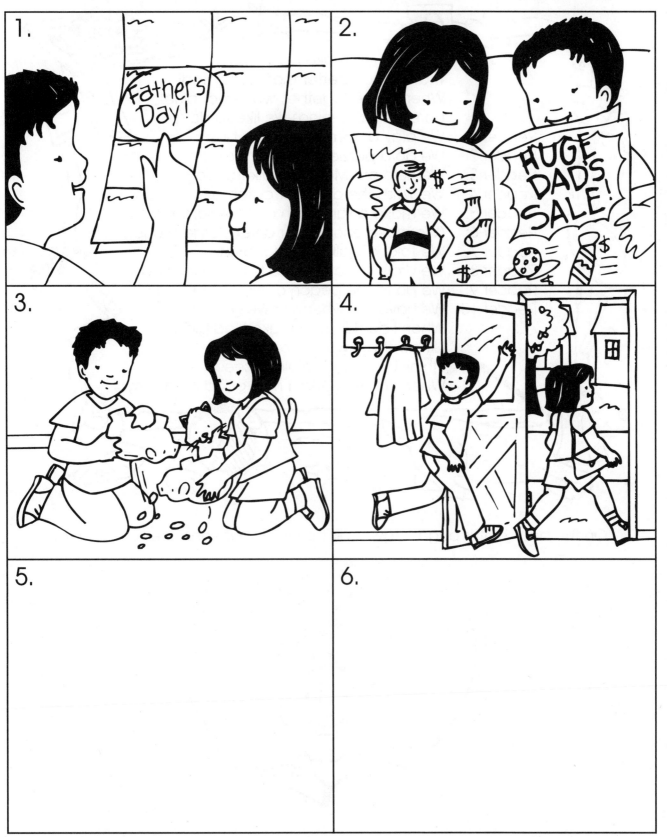

1.

2.

HUGE DAD'S SALE!

3.

4.

5.

6.

Name _____

Choral reading
Make Your Dad Glad!

All:	Isn't it fun to make Dad glad?
	That's much better than being sad!
	When we're together, we're not blue!
	Here's a list of things we like to do:
Reader 1:	We play a game or read a book.
Reader 2:	We do a puzzle or bait a hook.
Reader 3:	We help out Mom or walk the dog.
Reader 4:	We wash the dishes or catch a frog.
Reader 5:	We make a sandwich or cook some soup.
Reader 6:	(We make enough for a very large group.)
Reader 7:	We take a walk or go for a ride.
Reader 8:	We draw a picture and hang it with pride.
Reader 9:	We go to the beach or play in the snow.
Reader 10:	We have fun wherever we go.
All:	When I do things to make Dad glad,
	I know that I won't be sad.
	I think by now it's plain to see
	When I'm with Dad, I'm in good company!

On the back of this page, draw a picture to go with one line in the poem.

Solving a word search, identifying tools
Dad's Toolbox

Lots of fathers keep a box full of tools and parts so they can fix all sorts of things around the house. Here is a list of 21 different tools and supplies. Circle each word in the puzzle. The words may be spelled up, down, across or diagonally, both backwards and forwards.

Word List

hammer
screwdriver
tape measure
level
wrench
pliers
saw
nails
file
bolt
screws
nuts
wire
sandpaper
staple gun
sander
drill
chisel
plane
glue gun
clamp

S	A	W	N	U	T	S	H	E	L	I	F
T	C	X	U	Q	Z	S	C	R	E	W	S
A	S	R	G	V	K	O	N	L	S	M	A
P	L	I	E	R	S	N	E	E	A	R	N
L	I	W	U	W	O	T	R	S	N	M	D
E	A	I	L	C	D	E	W	I	D	L	P
G	N	R	G	L	M	R	E	H	E	L	A
U	P	E	E	M	A	N	I	C	R	I	P
N	U	V	A	S	A	B	G	V	I	R	E
O	E	H	E	L	T	L	O	B	E	D	R
L	T	A	P	E	M	E	A	S	U	R	E

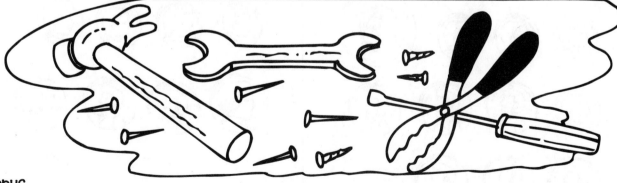

Bonus
If you're ready to work real hard, now put the words in ABC order. First number the words in ABC order, from 1 to 21. Then write the list on another piece of paper in the correct order.

Counting and writing money values
Father's Day Gifts
Find out how much each gift costs by counting and adding the coins.
Write the price in the box.

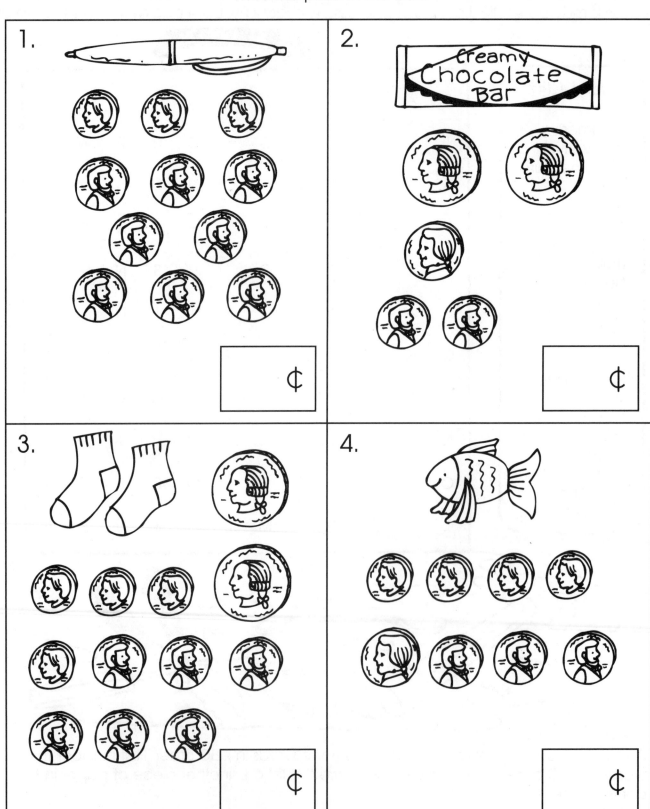

1.

¢

2.

Creamy Chocolate Bar

¢

3.

¢

4.

¢

Summer Vacation

Make the most of your students' excitement about summer vacation! Begin with this bulletin board idea, and then try some of the skill pages that follow.

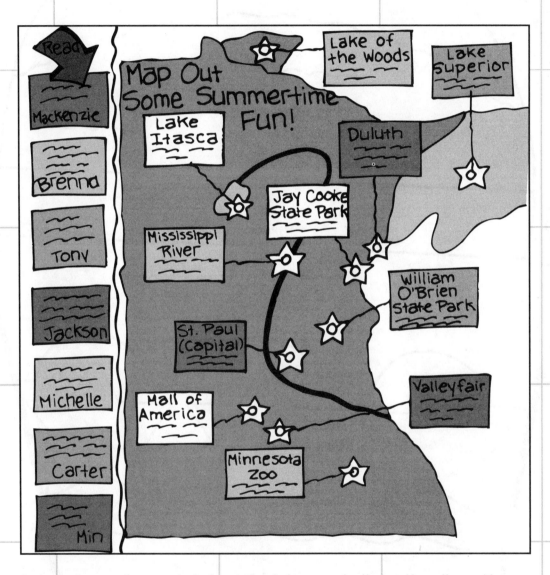

Label some of your state's parks, lakes and other attractions. Use yarn and pushpins to connect the site with its description. You may also wish to have students label places they plan to visit (or have already visited). They could write a sentence or two about the location on a 3" x 5" card, attach it to the board and label it with their name.

Shape Book Pattern

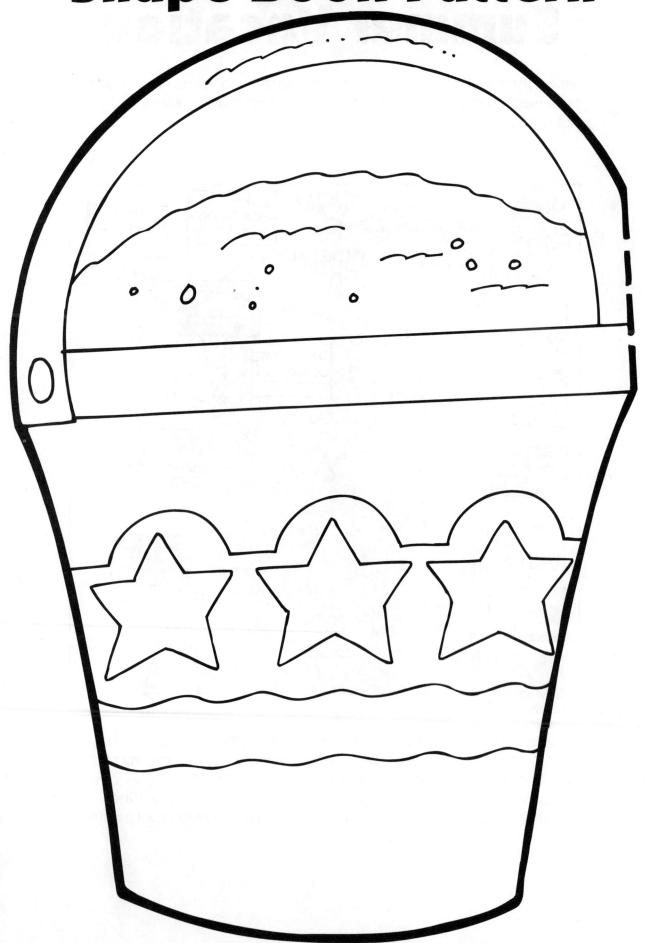

Name _____

Solving a maze
Beach Buddies

It's a long walk to the beach! Can you help Bryce find his buddy, Kyle,
who is waiting for him at the beach? Draw the path that Bryce should take.

Matching basic shapes

Road Signs

When you are traveling on vacation, you will see many road signs.
Look at the sign at the beginning of each row. Find the item in the row
that is the same shape and sign. Color the one that matches.

TLC10408 Copyright © Teaching & Learning Company, Carthage, IL 62321-0010

Name _____

Out of Order

The letters in each row are out of order. When you put them in the correct order, they will spell the name of one of the summertime pictures. Say the name of each picture. Find the row of letters for that picture. Number the boxes to put the letters in order. Then write each word, and cross out the picture after you use it. One is done for you.

1. a m p   <u>m a p</u>
   [2] [1] [3]

2. n a d s   _ _ _ _

3. l i p a   _ _ _ _

4. h i f s   _ _ _ _

5. n u s   _ _ _

6. a t b   _ _ _

7. l a b l   _ _ _ _

8. n e c o   _ _ _ _

9. t o b a   _ _ _ _

10. k e i b   _ _ _ _

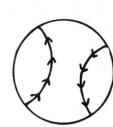

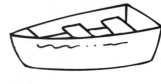

Name _____

Writing a narrative paragraph
You're a Writer

Read this paragraph that Kelsie wrote about her summer vacation:

This summer I learned to swim. I stayed with my cousin, Betsy, for one week. Her family has a swimming pool. At first I could not swim. But then Betsy taught me how. I'm so glad she taught me to swim!

A *paragraph* is a group of sentences that tell about one main idea. Kelsie's paragraph is a *narrative paragraph* because it tells about something someone did. You can write a narrative paragraph, too. Here's how:

• Choose a topic.
• Write one sentence that tells the main idea of your paragraph.
• Write more sentences that tell details about your topic.

Now it's your turn. Think about something you would like to do this summer. Write a narrative paragraph. Draw a picture to go with it.

_____

_____

_____

_____

_____

_____

_____

_____

_____

_____

Adjectives that tell how many
A Summer Description

Read this sentence that describes the Fishers' summer vacation:
This summer our family went to two campsites,
some state parks and every beach we could find!

In the sentence above, three words are used to tell *how many*. Can you find them? Write the word from the sentence above that answers each question:

How many campsites did we visit? _____

How many state parks did we see? _____

To how many beaches did we go? _____

Words that tell how many are adjectives. As you already know, adjectives can tell how big something is, what color it is, whether it's hot or cold or many other things. Adjectives can also tell how many. Words like *many, none* and *all* are adjectives. The words that answer the questions above are adjectives. Number words are adjectives, too.

Circle the adjective in each sentence that tells how many.

1. We saw some waterfalls on our vacation.

2. Every waterfall was beautiful!

3. Horseshoe Falls was the name of one waterfall.

4. Two other visitors did not know the name of the falls.

5. We gave them several flyers we had about the falls.

6. The waterfalls drop fifty feet.

7. Some people wanted to swim underneath the falls.

8. Few of us wanted to leave when it was time to go home.

9. Next summer, I hope we see many waterfalls!

Write two of your own sentences that contain adjectives that tell how many.
Use the back of this page.

Making change from one dollar

Time for Change

The Smith family has been shopping for vacation mementos.
Look at the price for each souvenir, and look at what someone paid for each item.
How much change should the person get?

1. 35¢   1 $ $ 1   _____ ¢

2. 89¢   1 $ $ 1   _____ ¢

3. 26¢   1 $ $ 1   _____ ¢

4. Tour Attractions   78¢   1 $ $ 1   _____ ¢

5. 65¢   1 $ $ 1   _____ ¢

6. 96¢   1 $ $ 1   _____ ¢

7. Black Bear Chocolate   55¢   1 $ $ 1   _____ ¢

Awards & Bookmarks

Award Certificates

This Special Achievement Award is hereby presented to

_____

for excellent work and conduct.

Congratulations!

**Best wishes
in all you do!**

Presented on   By

_____   _____

This Bicycle Safety Award goes to

_____

From _____

on

_____

Keep up the
safe riding!

An Outstanding Effort Award Goes
to

_____

for _____

Have a Great
Summer!

Teacher _____

Date _____

TLC10408 Copyright © Teaching & Learning Company, Carthage, IL 62321-0010

January

February

March

April

May

June

July Summer Vacation

Answer Key

January

A New Rhyme, page 12

"Hi, <u>Sue</u>!" said <u>Lou</u>. "What's <u>new</u> with <u>you</u>?"

The children were back at school after their winter holiday.

"<u>Lou</u>," said <u>Sue</u>, "I received the nicest gifts. Mom and Dad gave me a <u>blue</u> sweater. Gram gave me <u>two</u> free tickets <u>to</u> the zoo. Uncle Drew gave me the game, <u>Clue</u>™. <u>Do</u> <u>you</u> want <u>to</u> tell me what your family gave <u>to</u> <u>you</u>?

Before <u>Sue</u> could answer, their teacher asked them <u>to</u> line up <u>to</u> go <u>to</u> the library. Mrs. <u>Woo</u> said, "It's time <u>to</u> return our books today. Be sure <u>to</u> bring all of your library books with <u>you</u>. Some of <u>you</u> have some that are <u>overdue</u>. Before we leave, Kate, please <u>glue</u> the torn cover on your book. And, Alex, be sure <u>to</u> tie your left <u>shoe</u>."

Later that day <u>Sue</u> and <u>Lou</u> finished their chat about their holidays. Both agreed the <u>New</u> Year was off <u>to</u> a very good start.

New News! page 13

1. newspaper
2. newborn
3. newlywed
4. New Year's Day
5. newsletter
6. newcomer
7. New Jersey
8. newsprint
9. New Year's Eve
10. newscast

Oatmeal Energy! page 18

1. Beth
2. Jay
3. Mia
4. Dante

How Oatmeal Is Made, page 19

A. false	B. true	C. true
D. false	E. true	F. false
G. true	H. false	I. true

Tasty Toppings, page 21

18	walnuts	14	pears
7	figs	3	bananas
17	strawberries	5	cranberries
16	raisins	19	wheat germ
8	granola	20	yogurt
11	nectarines	6	dates
10	jam	13	pancake syrup
15	pineapple	2	apples
4	caramel	9	honey
1	almonds	12	oranges

More Tasty Toppings, page 22

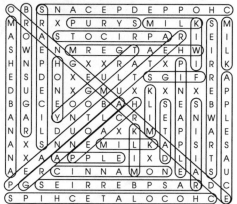

The word MILK appears five times.

Kitchen Math, page 25

1. a. 1 cup   b. 1 1/2 cups
   c. 2 cups   d. 3 cups
2. a. 2/3 cup   b. 1 cup   c. 1 2/3 cups
3. a. 7 cups   b. 10 1/2 cups

The Envelope, Please, page 34

Bryce Fisher
613 Ohboy St.
Mill Hall, PA 11111

Caleb Miller
897 Lee Avenue
Goshen, IN 40000

Just Because, page 40

1. b, c   2. a, b   3. a, c   4. a, b   5. a   6. b, c

A Busy Life, page 42

9, 2, 5, 3, 1, 6, 14, 8, 13, 4, 11, 12, 7, 10

Martin's March, pages 43-44

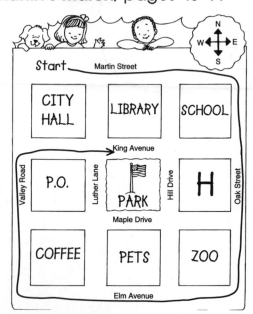

Answer Key

Noun Names, page 51

Some students may not find all the nouns in some sentences.

common nouns
1. inventor
3. lightning, electricity
4. eyeglasses
5. glasses, bifocals
6. stove
7. people, stove
8. stove, doors
9. stoves, stoves
10. heat, fireplace
11. reports, work
12. men, medal

proper nouns
1. Benjamin Franklin
2. Philadelphia, Pennsylvania
3. Ben
4. Franklin
6. Benjamin
7. America
9. Ben
11. Franklin, Britain
12. London, Ben

Franklin's Math, page 52

1. 29	2. okay	3. okay	4. 91
5. okay	6. 32	7. okay	8. 60
9. 41	10. 49	11. 78	12. okay
13. 91	14. 85	15. okay	16. 80

Winter Dot-to-Dot, page 59

It's an ice skate.

Spelling Riddle, page 60

Milk Shake

Animal Riddles, page 61

1. sheep or lamb	2. earthworm	3. fish
4. chicken	5. turtle	6. butterfly

Puzzling Math, page 62

1. 4 x 6 = 24   9 + 2 = 11
2. 12 ÷ 4 = 3   3 x 6 = 18   18 ÷ 2 = 9
3. 13 - 9 = 4   4 x 2 = 8   8 + 5 = 13
4. 7 x 6 = 42   42 - 10 = 32   32 ÷ 8 = 4   8 ÷ 4 = 2
5. 10 ÷ 2 = 5   5 - 5 = 0   3 x 9 = 27
6. 8 x 1 = 8   8 x 2 = 16   16 ÷ 4 = 4   4 ÷ 4 = 1
7. 11 x 2 = 22   22 - 10 = 12   12 ÷ 6 = 2

February

Harriet Tubman, page 70

1. E	2. F	3. B	4. H or C
5. A	6. C or H	7. G	8. D

Searching for Heroes, page 71

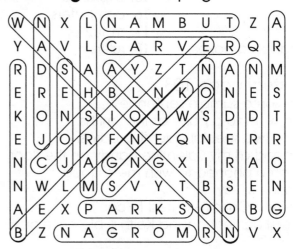

Ages and Stages, page 73

1. 1912- 1888 = 24
2. 1919-1913 = 6
3. 1929-1888 = 41
4. 1945-1919 = 26
5. 1947 + 12 = 1959
6. 1962 - 1919 = 43
7. 1940 + 11 = 1951
8. 1940 + 54 = 1994

Compound Animals, page 81

1. bobcat
2. sea horse
3. rattlesnake
4. guinea pig
5. goldfish
6. anteater
7. dragonfly
8. reindeer
9. sand crab

Groundhog Math, page 82

1. 3 + 2 = 5 □
2. 8 - 1 = 7 ⇦
3. 5 + 4 = 9 ✿
4. 9 - 1 = 8 ▲
5. 6 + 2 = 8 ▲
6. 7 - 6 = 1 ♡
7. 2 + 7 = 9 ✿
8. 9 - 5 = 4 ☽
9. 4 + 1 = 5 □
10. 8 - 3 = 5 □

Thomas Edison, page 88

1. 1879
2. 3 years (1882-1879)
3. no
4. phonograph
5. voting machine
6. He opened a laboratory at Menlo Park.
7. 84 years old (1931-1847)

Inventor at Work, page 91

3, 6, 1, 5, 8, 4, 9, 2, 7

Answer Key

Many Inventions! page 92

1. zippers
2. eyeglasses
3. papers
4. watches
5. pencils
6. wrenches
7. toasters
8. rockets
9. cardboard boxes
10. wheels
11. light switches
12. buttons
13. compasses
14. sandwiches
15. airplanes
16. computers
17. matches
18. rulers

Get Started! page 103

Here are some sample sentences:

1. Jason went to a party at the Smiths.
2. I made two special valentine cards.
3. I dropped all my valentine candy on the floor.
4. Grandma phoned to wish me a good Valentine's Day.
5. Dave and Carlos wanted to cook.
6. The mail carrier handed Keith a big envelope.

Valentine Riddle, page 105

I love you a ton!

Middle Math, page 106

Sample answers include:

1. Jose took 11 cupcakes.
2. Alex made 8 more cards.
3. Jawan spent 35¢ on milk.
4. Her sister gave her 5 stickers.
5. She also asked 9 students to clean tables.
6. On Tuesday the mailman brought 6 more valentines.

Lost and Found, page 110

1. to the flag
2. crafts
3. first aid
4. books

Abraham Lincoln, page 111

1. was
2. grew
3. worked
4. loved, loved
5. held
6. became
7. enjoy
8. lives
9. loves
10. are

President Cents, page 113

2. 31¢
3. 60¢
4. 71¢
5. 60¢
6. $2.04
7. $1.50
8. $1.62
9. $3.00
10. 98¢

Hidden President, page 114

John Adams

Pancake Breakfast! page 118

1. Thursday and Friday, February 27th and 28th
2. 7 a.m. to 9 a.m.
3. blueberry pancakes, apple pancakes, sausage and bacon
4. orange juice, grape juice, milk
5. give it to the City Homeless Shelter
6. - 7. Answers will vary.

Pancake Party, page 119

1. yes
2. no
3. you can't tell
4. no
5. you can't tell
6. yes

How Many Pancakes? page 121

1. 8 apples
2. 12 tablespoons
3. 1 cup
4. 4 cups
5. 50 plates
6. 48 cups
7. 30 glasses
8. 27 pancakes

March

The Umbrella, page 134

The umbrella has two main uses. <u>First</u>, many people use it to keep <u>rain</u> off and stay dry. Secondly, some people use it to keep the heat of the <u>sun</u> off.

At first, umbrella frames were made of <u>wood</u>, and they were covered by cloth or animal <u>skin</u>. Now, frames are usually <u>made</u> of metal, and they may be covered with cloth or plastic.

Hundreds of years <u>ago</u>, in some countries, only the priests and ministers carried <u>umbrellas</u>. Later in <u>other</u> countries, only ladies carried umbrellas. These umbrellas were called <u>parasols</u>.

Now almost every <u>family</u> has one or more umbrellas, and we are all <u>thankful</u> for this invention, especially on a very rainy or very hot <u>day</u>!

Subtract and Color, page 138

Students should color two umbrellas.

Pigpen, page 141

2. run, rag, red
3. leg, lid, lot
4. jam, jug, jar
5. map, mud, mob
6. sun, sat, sip
7. hot, his, ham
8. yet, yes, yam
9. not, nap, net
10. wig, wag, was
11. ten, tar, tip
12. big, bag, bug

Where's the Pig? page 143

(Variations are possible.)

1. in
2. under
3. on
4. across
5. to
6. around

TLC10408 Copyright © Teaching & Learning Company, Carthage, IL 62321-0010

Answer Key

Hungry Animals, page 147
1. rabbit, sheep   2. lion   3. bird

Ready, Set, Go! page 153
Set 3 is the correct set.

Eye Exam, page 154
A. 3, 7   B. 11, 15   C. 4, 8   D. 2, 5, 9   E. 6, 10

Lucky Hats, page 161
Lucky's hat is F.

Irish Cities, page 163
5, 1, 9, 3, 8, 2, 13, 12, 4, 14, 11, 7, 6, 10

A Lucky Day, page 164
1. sandy   2. slippery   3. cold
4. long   5. good   6. dry
7. blazing, hot   8. cozy   9. fun

Leprechaun Languages, page 165
1. green   2. lucky   3. girl   4. gold
5. sheep   6. Irish   7. boy   8. snack
9. green   10. fun

Party Preparations, page 166
1. 2 extra cups   2. 8 extra cookies
3. 56 utensils in all (28 knives plus 28 spoons)
4. 9 jars of paint   5. 4 extra bottles
6. 6 extra balloons   7. 11 more shamrocks
8. 7 minutes

Kite Flight, page 168
1. green   2. red   3. yellow   4. blue

Kite Chaos, page 170

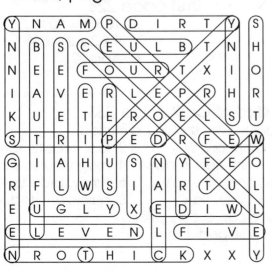

Ducklings, page 175
1. $7 + 6 = 13$ 2. $5 + 6 = 11$
   $6 + 7 = 13$ $6 + 5 = 11$
   $13 - 7 = 6$ $11 - 6 = 5$
   $13 - 6 = 7$ $11 - 5 = 6$
3. $8 + 4 = 12$ 4. $6 + 9 = 15$
   $4 + 8 = 12$ $9 + 6 = 15$
   $12 - 4 = 8$ $15 - 6 = 9$
   $12 - 8 = 4$ $15 - 9 = 6$

How Many Bubbles? page 180
20

Bubble Math 1, page 183
Variations are possible.
1. $3 + 2 = 5$ 2. $7 + 1 = 8$ 3. $9 + 0 = 9$
4. $6 + 4 = 10$ 5. $5 + 8 = 13$

Bubble Math 2, page 184
Any arrangement will work in which opposite bubbles total 10.

April

Trash Can Families, page 203
Here are some possible answers:
2. ran, ban, fan, man, pan, tan, van
3. bake, lake, make, wake, fake, sake, rake, ache
4. bat, cat, mat, pat, fat, flat, sat
5. ring, sing, ding, sling, bring, king
6. band, hand, sand, brand
7. drink, sink, link, mink, kink, rink
8. green, seen, lean, mean, wean, keen
9. pain, cane, dane, gain, lane, rain, brain, drain

America the Beautiful, page 204
1. happy   2. young   3. short
4. asleep   5. near   6. many
7. none   8. never   9. quick
10. stand   11. large   12. light
13. leave   14. right   15. under

Nature Walk, page 205
   Mr. Tyler's <u>class</u> went on a nature walk. First they walked through the playground. Then they crossed the <u>street</u>. Finally, the students began walking on a <u>trail</u> in the woods.
   "Tell me what you see," said Mr. Tyler.
   "I see a tall <u>pine</u> tree," reported Bryce.
   "<u>Look</u>! There's a butterfly!" exclaimed Betsy.
   "I see three baby <u>robins</u> in a nest in that tree," said Amy.

Answer Key

There were so many beautiful things to see in the woods. Steve saw some <u>purple</u> wildflowers. Kelsie saw some wiggly <u>worms</u>. Kyle thought he saw a <u>gopher</u> running across the ground. Rob noticed a maple tree with tiny new <u>leaves</u>.

At the end of their walk, Mr. Tyler asked a tricky <u>question</u>. "What didn't you see?" he asked. "It's something I was hoping we would not see, and we didn't!"

The students thought and thought. At last Rob raised his <u>hand</u>.

"I know, Mr. Tyler! We didn't see any <u>litter</u>!" he shouted.

All at once, everyone knew Rob was <u>right</u>. Everyone cheered.

Best Guess, page 206
1. a   2. b   3. b   4. b   5. a   6. b   7. a
8. b   9. b

Garbage Trucks, page 207
Jed-182, Ned-176, Ted-192, Redd-176.
Ted's truck should be circled because he had the highest total.
Ned and Redd's trucks should be colored because they had the same total.

Rosa's Route, page 209
1. Hart   2. Jones   3. Hart
4. south   5. east   6. north

Earth Search, page 210
Here are the words students should locate:
1. rainy, sunny, windy
2. newspapers, plastic jugs, cans, glass
3. flowers, trees, seeds
4. robin
5. butterfly, bee
6. kittens, calves, lambs

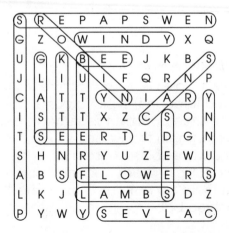

Trick the Teacher, page 217
1. Because he tricked them first by pretending to be absent.
2. To pretend to be the substitute teacher.
3. Ronnie
4. Both were good tricks, because no one would be hurt, etc.
5. They may have been laughing at Mr. Smith's joke. Some may have been disappointed that he tricked them first, and so on.

Tricky Students, page 218
A. Leo   B. Nick   C. Jana

The Long Way, page 220
These lines are the longest: 1. C   2. A   3. B

Was It Real? page 223
1. N   2. F   3. N   4. F   5. F
6. N   7. N   8. F   9. F   10. N

Authors' Order, page 224
Here are the authors' last names in ABC order:
1. Dime   2. Dirty   3. Doe   4. Hanks
5. Happy   6. Honest   7. Match   8. Pets
9. Princess   10. Two

Program Notes, page 226
1. .   2. ?   3. .   4. ?   5. .
6. ?   7. .   8. .   9. .   10. ?

Check It Out! page 227
1. 30   2. 41   3. 27   4. 31
5. 82   6. 102   7. 101   8. 71
9. 143   10. 103

That's Not So Fine! page 228
1. 4 x 3 = 12¢   2. 10 x 3 = 30¢
3. 12 x 3 = 36¢   4. 9 x 3 x 2 = 54¢
5. 16 x 3 = 48¢   6. April 22
7. 5 x 4 x 3 = 60¢

What Kind of Cat? page 233
These adjectives should be circled.
1. quick, hungry, tiny   2. lazy, woolly, soft
3. wet, feathered, brown   4. tough, quiet, slippery
5. small, noisy, friendly   6. funny, proud, white
7. sticky, slimy, slow   8. quick, spotted, wild
9. dangerous, green, prickly
10. smelly, striped, black

TLC10408 Copyright © Teaching & Learning Company, Carthage, IL 62321-0010

Answer Key

Pet Shop, page 234
Row 1: 11   Row 2: 12   Row 3: 15

Pet Shop Prices, page 235
1. 4 + 15 + 7 = $26
2. 12 + 1 + 13 + 2 = $28
3. 16 + 9 + 7 = $32
4. 16 + 1 + 18 + 18 + 15 + 20 = $88
5. 20 + 21 + 18 + 11 + 5 + 25 = $100
6. 13 + 15 + 21 + 19 + 5 = $73
7. 19 + 14 + 1 + 11 + 5 = $50
8. 3 + 18 + 1 + 2 = $24
The crab costs the least. The turkey costs the most.

Easter Egg Hunt, page 240
F and G are the same.

Easter Baskets, page 241
Multiples of 5: 5, 10, 20, 30
Odd numbers: 7, 13, 19, 27
Numbers larger than 30: 31, 36, 42, 54

Summer

Bike Quiz, page 249
1. C   2. A   3. C   4. B   5. B
6. C   7. A   8. C   9. A   10. B

Let's Think, page 252
1. apple   2. hand   3. ears   4. cub
5. snow   6. book   7. bird   8. pond

Barb's Bicycle, page 250

Bicycle Shop, page 253
1. 4   2. 24   3. 2   4. 3   5. 19

Riding Riddle, page 254
Because it is too (2) tired!

Look-Alikes, page 257
B and E are the same.

Hey Diddle, Diddle! page 258
2 - The cow jumped over the moon.
4 - The dish ran away with the spoon.
1 - The cat and the fiddle.
3 - The little dog laughed to see such a sport.

Ready for Action, page 259
Correct matches and action verbs:
1. J, sat   2. H, played   3. F, jumped
4. L, lost   5. D, ate   6. A, followed
7. K, met   8. G, sat   9. E, walked
10. C, lived   11. B, ran   12. I, ran

Mother Goose Math, page 260
1. 6 + 8 + 5, 19   2. 3 x 2, 6
3. 3 x 7, 21   4. 5 x 4, 20
5. 4 + 7 + 3, 14   6. 12 - 9, 3
7. 17 - 6, 11   8. 63 + 63 (or 63 x 2), 126
9. 9 x 4, 36
10. 100 - 89, 11¢ (or $1.00 - $0.89 = $0.11)

Hidden Picture, page 262
The uncolored spaces will reveal a sombrero.

Scrambled Colors, page 263
1. red   2. blue   3. green   4. white
5. yellow   6. purple   7. brown

May Flowers, page 267
1. B   2. M   3. E   4. B   5. M
6. E   7. B   8. E   9. M   10. B
11. M   12. B   13. E   14. M   15. B
16. E   17. M   18. E   19. B   20. E

Mother's Work, page 268
Sentences should be similar to these:
1. That is Pam's brush.
2. The slippers are Jill's.
3. That is Sally's rolling pin.
4. Those are Deb's X rays.
5. The rope is Mary's.

Mothers on Parade, page 269

Answer Key

Mother's Day Gifts, page 270
2. HUGS   3. RING   4. ROSES   5. DRESS
6. MUSIC   7. DINNER   8. PICTURE   9. LOVE

Get a Group! page 275
Correct categories are listed, along with possible additions to each group. Students' additions may vary.
2. American symbols; the White House, Mount Rushmore, etc.
3. Songs; "The Star-Spangled Banner," "You're a Grand Old Flag," etc.
4. U.S. States; Michigan, Ohio, Alaska, etc.
5. Presidents; Clinton, Reagan, Adams, Jefferson, etc.
6. sounds; zap, whiz, etc.

Patriotic Parade, page 276
(Variations may be possible.)
All the children in town were ready for the big parade. They had washed their bikes until the bikes were shiny. They decorated the bikes with colors from the flag. Then they dressed in their best clothes. The children stood under the shady tree while they waited for the parade to start.

At last the parade began. The leaders of the parade were the fire trucks with their noisy sirens. Next came the soldiers in their green uniforms. Last came the children with their fancy bikes.

At the end of the parade, some very kind ladies waited with cold ice cream cones! All the children agreed that was a wonderful surprise.

Measure Up! page 277
1. 3"   2. 3"   3. 5"   4. 1"   5. 6"

Fast 50, page 278
These items should be crossed out:
Row 1: B, C   Row 2: B, D   Row 3: none
Row 4: A, C   Row 5: B

Get in Shape, page 281
4 diamonds, 6 squares, 9 triangles, 17 circles

Have a Ball! page 284
1. donut   2. plate   3. wheel
4. circle   5. pizza   6. clock
7. nickel   8. button   9. snowball

Little League Logic, page 285
1. shortstop
2. Eagles (Each of the other teams must have received four votes.)

3. yes
4. no
5. Marco is the fourth boy.

Team Totals, page 286
The Eagles were the winners.

	1	2	3	4	5	6	7	Total
Eagles	2	0	0	3	4	2	1	12
Tigers	2	1	1	3	0	3	0	10

Dad's Toolbox, page 291

In ABC order:
1. bolt   2. chisel   3. clamp
4. drill   5. file   6. glue gun
7. hammer   8. level   9. nails
10. nuts   11. plane   12. pliers
13. sander   14. sandpaper   15. saw
16. screwdriver 17. screws   18. staple gun
19. tape measure 20. wire   21. wrench

Father's Day Gifts, page 292
1. 38¢   2. 57¢   3. 96¢   4. 48¢

A Summer Description, page 299
1. some   2. Every   3. one   4. Two
5. several 6. fifty   7. Some   8. Few
9. many

Time for Change, page 300
1. 65¢ 2. 11¢ 3. 74¢ 4. 22¢ 5. 35¢ 6. 4¢ 7. 45¢

TLC10408 Copyright © Teaching & Learning Company, Carthage, IL 62321-0010

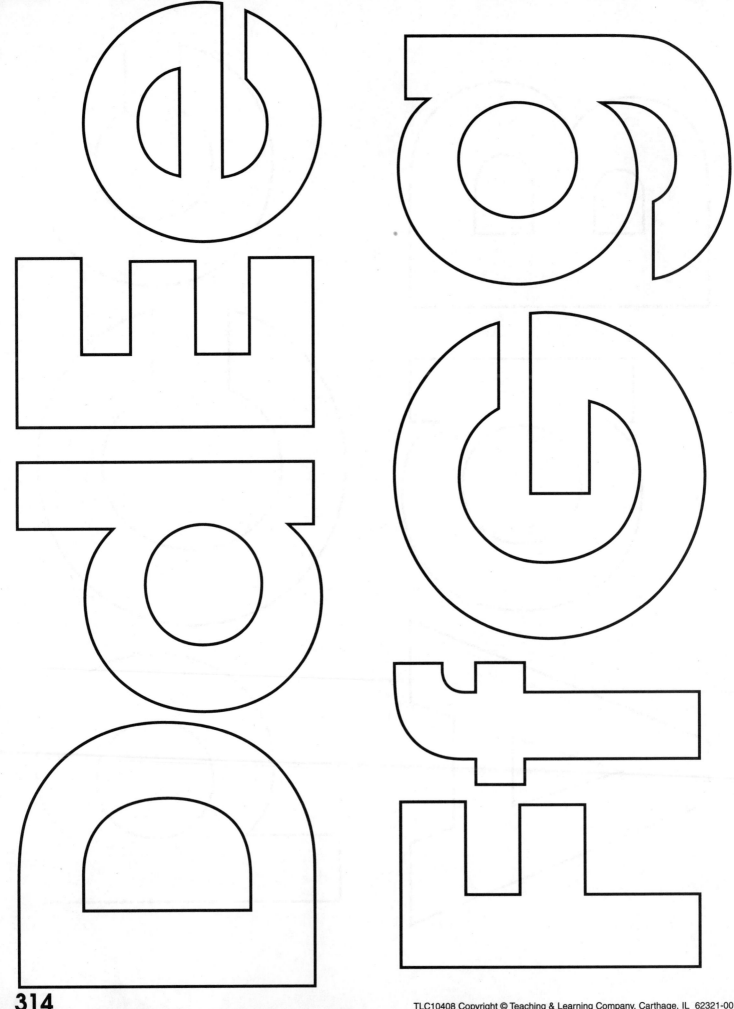

316

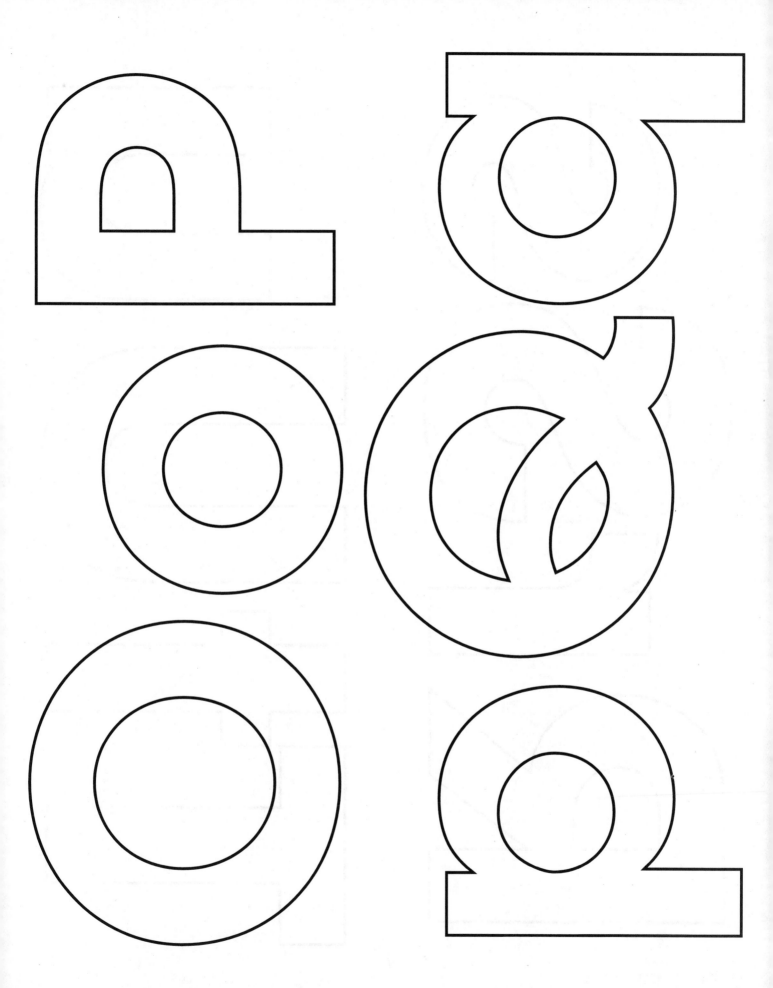

318

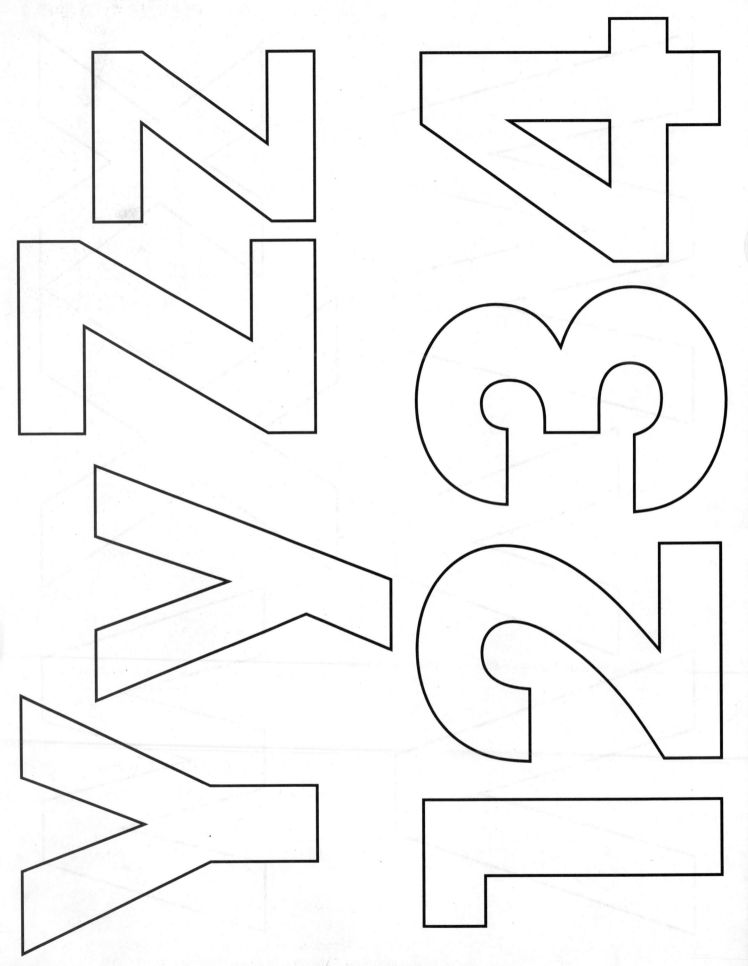

320